THE FAR-AWAY DREAM
My Vietnam Memoir

David A. Crum

authorHOUSE

AuthorHouse™
1663 Liberty Drive
Bloomington, IN 47403
www.authorhouse.com
Phone: 1 (800) 839-8640

© 2018 David A. Crum. All rights reserved.

No part of this book may be reproduced, stored in a retrieval system, or transmitted by any means without the written permission of the author.

Published by AuthorHouse 02/22/2018

ISBN: 978-1-5462-2488-4 (sc)
ISBN: 978-1-5462-2486-0 (hc)
ISBN: 978-1-5462-2487-7 (e)

Library of Congress Control Number: 2018900555

Print information available on the last page.

Any people depicted in stock imagery provided by Thinkstock are models, and such images are being used for illustrative purposes only. Certain stock imagery © Thinkstock.

This book is printed on acid-free paper.

Because of the dynamic nature of the Internet, any web addresses or links contained in this book may have changed since publication and may no longer be valid. The views expressed in this work are solely those of the author and do not necessarily reflect the views of the publisher, and the publisher hereby disclaims any responsibility for them.

Scripture taken from the NEW AMERICAN STANDARD BIBLE®, Copyright © 1960, 1962, 1963, 1968, 1971, 1972, 1973, 1975, 1977, 1995 by the Lockman Foundation. Used by permission. www.Lockman.org

Dedication

This book is dedicated to the wives of pastors, chaplains, campus ministers, and all whose husbands labor in full-time ministry. It is dedicated to my wife and teacher of our children Jill Crum, to Marjorie Cunningham, to Mary Lee Bayly, to Elsie Ellsworth, to Kathy Nussbaum, to Bonnie Abboud, to Sarah Benner, to Erica Herron, to Caroline Tubbesing, to Amy Holdeman, to Anne Niess, to Melinda Von Bokern, to Gladys Crouthamel, to Barbara Riches, to Lisa Hicks and especially to Mrs. Jack Stafford – my pastor's wife and my spiritual mother.

Acknowledgements

I mention in the text of the book how grateful I am to LtCol. Jim Spangler for his advice that I speak often of my Vietnam experiences to the Marines at the Infantry Training School at Camp Pendleton. That advice resulted in my relating these experiences not only to the ITS Marines, but also to members of the various congregations I have served as well as to anyone who has been willing to listen. In the writing of the book I have greatly benefitted from the suggestions of my daughter-in-law, Michal Bayly Crum, my son Matthew, and my son Benjamin (Michal's husband). The portrait photo on the back cover was taken by my daughter-in-law Katie Crum. The illustrations were drawn by my wife Jill, our sons Peter, Benjamin, Nathaniel (Katie's husband) and William, and by our grandsons, Daniel and Zion. The cover photo was taken by a Marine photographer during the Battle of Hue. Benjamin designed the book cover and also provided the publication of this book by AuthorHouse. My thanks to Rowella, Joey, Sandy, Ben and all at AuthorHouse who provided their professional assistance.

Contents

Dedication v
Acknowledgements vii
Preface xi

Life before the Marine Corps 1
The Marine Corps 13
Vietnam 33
Life after Vietnam 93

Postlude 109
Glossary 113

Preface

"For I know the plans I have for you," declares the L*ord*, *"plans to prosper you and not to harm you, plans to give you hope and a future."*

— Jeremiah 29:11

It all seems like a far-away dream. You might think I should say nightmare. But it is so far away that the disturbing nightmares have ceased and, for the most part, I have stopped crying when I talk about it. So, it is more like a dream. And more like a dream than a memory, because, although I can remember details quite well, it is hard for me to believe I actually experienced the things I remember.

I must admit the horror I experienced has all but been erased from my memory. I thank the Lord for this and I give a lot of the credit to advice I was given a little over twelve years after I had been honorably discharged from the Marine Corps.

I had received an appointment as a Lieutenant Junior Grade (Lieutenant JG) in the Chaplain Corps of the U S Navy in July 1982 and had reported to the Infantry Training School (ITS) at Camp Pendleton Marine Corps Base in September. During my welcome interview with the Executive Officer of ITS, Lieutenant Colonel Jim Spangler, we discussed my combat experience in Vietnam. Without the least bit of hesitation, Colonel Spangler exhorted me (encouraged, advised, counseled – pick the verb) to speak often of my experiences to the young Marines I would encounter, and to describe these experiences in vivid detail.

I didn't know at the time that this is something combat veterans seldom do, unless they are talking to other combat veterans. I since have met combat veterans, and I have heard of many others, who never, or almost never, talk about their combat experiences. And too many of these continue to suffer as they live with the horrors they witnessed.

Thanks to Colonel Spangler I did tell those young Marines about my combat experiences, then I told older Marines, then sailors, then the people in the churches I have served. My children have heard many of my "stories"; but when I hear them repeat them, the details are often confused. And so, I decided to take Colonel Spangler's "advice" one step further, and record those accounts in written form.

And, so, here are my horror stories with most of the horror missing, though I tell the stories the way I remember them. I am no longer haunted by them, although I still sometimes begin to cry while I'm relating them. I see them now with a much different lens than I did while I was living them. I see now how the Lord's hand was upon me then and how He has used these events and how He continues to use them in my life and in the lives of others who hear them. May you "hear" them and be drawn by the Lord to the kind of love and reverence that I have for Him – for the living God: Father, Son and Holy Spirit.

First Baptist Church, Rochester by Peter Crum

Chapter One

Life before the Marine Corps

And we know that God causes all things to work together for good to those who love God, to those who are called according to His purpose.

– Romans 8:28

Rochester is a common name for a town. There is Rochester, Minnesota and Rochester, New York and a host of others. I was born in an unknown, unremarkable Rochester: Rochester, Pennsylvania. It is located on the Ohio River about 25 miles west of where the Ohio is formed in Pittsburgh. I was the sixth of eight children born to my father Bill and my mother Mary (William and Mary, you know like the King and Queen and the college in Virginia). Barbara was the oldest, followed by Bob, Judy, Frances, Billy, me, Debbie and Pam.

My father was the youngest of seven children born to George Ira and Sarah Crum. There were two sets of boy/girl twins in his family – Earl and Pearl, and Lawrence and Florence. I never met Pearl or an older sister, Edith. Both had died before I was born. Each had children who were older than my dad and still, I'm told, when they were young they referred to their younger uncle as Uncle William Henry. Another sister, Mary, was just a couple of years older than my father. She was his one sibling I knew well.

My mother was one of five children. She was born in Oklahoma, but was raised in western Pennsylvania. Because her father was a gambler, there were times when the children lived either with an aunt and uncle or they lived in a children's home. Things were not much better for my mother as a wife. My father was a laborer on the Pennsylvania Railroad. He was a hard worker, but he could also be a heavy drinker. All too often he came home on payday drunk and broke. This was especially hard on my mother and oldest siblings. My older brother Bob got his driver's license when he was 16 so that when my dad was brought home drunk by a friend, Bob could hitchhike to wherever Dad had left the car and drive it home. Mom often depended on her brother Paul and her sisters, Mildred (Mid) and Florence, to help pay the bills. Food was supplemented with cheese and powdered milk from welfare. As one of the younger children, I kind of took it in stride; although, I admit, I never did learn to like the powdered milk.

The Far-Away Dream

Still, I enjoyed my childhood: playing baseball with the neighborhood boys just about every day in the summer, playing football in nearby fields in the fall, playing basketball on driveways and in gyms in the winter. Life was good. I even liked school; and I did well in school. As early as third grade, whenever my class had a test, my teacher, Miss Cable, would correct my test first so that she could give me the job of grading my classmates' tests.

We moved a lot when I was young. We lived in seven homes by the time I was ten. My father, who always rented homes, was an excellent handyman. He could fix practically anything that needed fixing. I don't know this for a fact, but I have always suspected that we would move into a house that was desperately in need of repair, my dad would make the repairs, the rent would be raised, and we would have to move. At any rate, we kept moving until I was ten, then my parents bought a house. No more moving!

The first place I lived was in a housing project in the town of Baden. From Baden we moved to Freedom, overlooking the Pennsylvania Railroad (PRR), Jones and Laughlin (J & L) Steel Mill and the Ohio River. We lived in Conway, not far from the Conway Yard freight yards of the railroad, when I entered first grade. Before I had completed first grade we moved in with my father's mother in Rochester. In the next three years, we lived in three houses in Rochester, first my grandmother's house following the death of my grandfather, and then two more, one on Jackson Street that was connected to the Knights of Columbus hall and one on Pinny Street across from the hospital in which I was born. Finally, we bought a house outside of New Brighton in the country.

Living in town, as we did in Rochester, makes it easier gathering enough friends to play baseball. In the country, there were not so many boys. As a result, we often played games with fewer players, so that the right-handed batters had to hit to the left side of the field and the left-handed batters had to hit to the right. But, as they say, where there's a will there's a way. We made do. Nothing was going to stop my brother Bill and me from playing baseball. We even devised a way to play baseball in our basement (long before "Wii" was invented).

Because we were buying a house and monthly payments had to be made, Dad brought his pay – or at least a good portion of it – home most paydays once we had moved to New Brighton. Life in our home was considerably "safer" during my teen years than it had been for my older siblings during their teen years. But, since I had never had any money to spend, I didn't need much. I had friends, I had sports and I had school. What else did I need?

I also had my church. Little did I know how much I needed that.

The Far-Away Dream

We attended the First Baptist Church in Rochester. This had been my father's family's church for years and years. Throughout my younger years, we would attend Sunday school and worship almost every Sunday. This, of course, was easier to do once we moved to Rochester. We could walk to the church. However, when I was in high school, my parents stopped going on a regular basis. They never said why; and I don't believe I ever asked them. I still wanted to go; so, since I didn't drive, and since we lived outside of New Brighton and the church was at least five miles away in Rochester, I would hitch-hike to church each Sunday: twice each Sunday; once on Sunday morning, and then again Sunday evening for Baptist Youth Fellowship. I occasionally got a ride from a neighbor who attended the same church; but his attendance was not very good. Other than him, I don't remember anyone else offering to give me a ride. So, I hitch-hiked.

I had grown up in that church. Most of my Sunday school classmates and I had attended together since we were carried there as babies. My attachment to them and to my church was strong; and, though I may not have been able to articulate it at the time, I believe I already possessed a deep and genuine faith in Jesus Christ. I recall sitting in a Sunday school class when I first came home on leave from the Marine Corps (just prior to going to Vietnam). Several of my classmates were also there, home for the weekend from college.

I was shocked to hear a couple of them questioning theological issues such as the virgin birth of Christ and His bodily resurrection from the dead. When I was asked what I thought, I fervently stood by both. There was no question in my mind that Jesus is God in the flesh, born of the virgin Mary, and that following His death on the cross, He was raised again. His disciples saw a physical Jesus; not an apparition. I was going to Vietnam with the solid conviction that I had eternal life; that, like Christ, when I would die, I would also be raised to life in a real, physical body. I wondered if going to college might make people stupid.

As God would have it (and as He planned it), our church called a new pastor as I was entering my teen years. Pastor Jack Stafford was a solid evangelical, Bible-believing pastor. He and his family had a tremendous influence on my life. (More about this later.) I spent time in the Stafford home and was especially influenced by the enthusiastic love for Christ (and for me) of Mrs. Stafford. In our home, we only prayed together as a family once a week – at dinner on Sunday. We never read the Bible, we never sang hymns, we never did any kind of spiritual activity (except for prayer at Sunday dinner). In the Stafford home, there was prayer often and we even stood around the piano singing hymns as Mrs. Stafford joyfully pounded out a tune. I think it was here I was introduced to the idea of praying at all times.

The Far-Away Dream

This would become my practice in Marine Corps boot camp and in Vietnam.

Having Pastor Stafford and his family at our church and in my life, was certainly one of the things God provided to prepare me for what I would encounter in the Marine Corps. Two other things were the games I played during my childhood and the sport I participated in during my last two years of high school.

I was seven years old when we moved in with my grandmother in Rochester. Her house was on the edge of a residential neighborhood and a very large wooded area. For the next three years in Rochester and for the following years in New Brighton (there was an even larger wooded area behind our home there) I played in those woods either with others or by myself. Most often I played what I called "war". I played as if I was in combat. I ran through the woods. I hid behind trees and in trenches. I crawled along the ground. I experienced a kind of infantry training from the time I was 10 until I was 17 or 18. When I got to infantry training in the Marine Corps I was already familiar with many of the activities of a "grunt".

Although I had played baseball as a young boy, I never became a very good baseball player. By the time I was in high school my favorite sport was basketball. I thought I was pretty good and I certainly thought I had the potential to be better with the coaching and experience I could receive. But I was not very tall and

I was very skinny. I did not play beyond my sophomore year, and I didn't play much then either, even though I was on the Junior Varsity team.

I wanted to play some sport. (I had always dreamed of going to the Naval Academy and I thought it would help my chances of getting into the academy if I would letter in a sport.) I was too thin and too weak for football (although I regarded myself as probably the best quarterback in my school). I was a lousy golfer (little did I know that most of the other golfers on the golf team were also lousy golfers). I was not too great at tennis – a gross understatement. What sport could I try? My brother Bill and I had tried track when he was a senior and I was a freshman. We didn't last long. But that was two years earlier. I decided to give track another try.

Since I didn't have the skills for any of the field events, like throwing the discus or shot put, or high jumping or long jumping or pole vaulting; and since I was not fast enough for any of the sprints; it seemed my only option was distance running, and, since I was slow, the longer the distance the better. The longest distance was the two mile. I became a two-miler. I wasn't the best two-miler, not even on our team. Tom Kopriva was the best two-miler on our team and one of the best in our county. I could never keep up with him. Nevertheless, I was our #2 two-miler and I could often beat the #2 two-miler on other teams and sometimes their #1; so, I did letter in track.

But why would I enlist in the Marine Corps? I was a good student. Why wouldn't I go to college?

I wanted to go to college. I specifically wanted to attend the Naval Academy and become a Navy officer. Between my sophomore and junior years, I contacted my U. S. Congressman and both U. S. Senators from Pennsylvania, seeking their sponsorship so that I could take the written exam for the Naval Academy. I received two letters, one from my Congressman and one from one of the Senators. I took the exam. As it turned out, I took the exam one year too soon; for, although I was an excellent math student, I had not yet studied trigonometry. Much of the math on the exam was trigonometry. My performance suffered. My grade was not high enough. The next year I took the exam for Naval Reserve Officer Training Corps (NROTC). This wouldn't have gotten me into the Academy, but it would have provided a full scholarship to a university. I did very well on the exam (thanks to the fact that I had mastered trigonometry); but when I underwent the physical exam, it was discovered that I was partially color-blind. I was informed that this disqualified me from becoming a Navy officer. And so, even if I had done well on the Naval Academy exam, I still would not have received an appointment.

Because I was good at math Mr. Donnelly, my physics teacher, and Mr. Fischer, my geometry and trigonometry teacher, encouraged me to take the test for a math scholarship to nearby Westminster College. They were doing their best to help me get into college. However, that test was being administered on the same day as the exam for NROTC. I took the latter test. As I said, I did well enough on the test, but failed the entrance physical because I was partially color-blind. This left me with no scholarship and no way, that I knew of, to go to college. Before long, I would find myself in the United States Marine Corps, color-blind or not.

The Rochester Post Office by Ben Crum

Chapter Two

The Marine Corps

The mind of man plans his way, but the Lord directs his steps.

— Proverbs 16:9

Enlisting: "The Marine Corps builds men."

I was 18 when I went to Vietnam. After just a few weeks I turned 19. I am now 68. It was a long, long time ago. The year was 1968. I had just graduated from high school in June of 1967. A year earlier I would have been sitting in history or physics or English class. I might have had lunch at the Brighton Hot Dog Shop – the real one, the original one in downtown New Brighton. I would have been in training for the Spring track season. But now I spent my days and nights in the heat and humidity – you know, like 100% humidity – of South Vietnam.

To tell you the truth, I shouldn't have been in Vietnam. No, really! Mr. Donnelly, my physics teacher and track coach, had given me information about an apprentice program at nearby St. Joe Lead. St. Joe Lead was one of the many mills along the Ohio River, west of Pittsburgh. It specialized in producing metallic zinc and zinc oxide. (It had originally been a large producer of lead; thus, its name.) I had followed up on Mr. Donnelly's suggestion, applied, been tested, and had been hired. It was a four-year apprenticeship that included an exemption from the draft (my dad's dream for me come true). I began a week after graduation.

Since St. Joe was not a union mill, we worked six days a week and sometimes seven. I was just out of high school and I was working six or seven days a week. I have never been good with my hands. Whenever my dad did home improvements, I helped him – I handed him the tools, but I seldom used them myself. When I was twelve I entered the soap box derby. I built one of the largest, bulkiest racers on record. If the bosses at St. Joe Lead had seen my racer, they would never have hired me. And yet here I was an apprentice and a full-time worker at St. Joe. In January of 1968 when I first arrived in Vietnam, I should have been in the metal shop or electrician shop or one of the other shops in which the apprentices worked. Instead, in July of 1967, only a few weeks after I started at St. Joe, I had had enough of the dirt, fumes, heat and my own awkwardness with the tools and machines; I asked Mr. Ruby (who lived nearby and gave me a ride to and from work, since he also worked at St. Joe) to drop me off at the post office in Rochester. He didn't ask me why and I didn't tell him. It was only a block or two out of our way and he simply did what I asked and dropped me off there. I doubt if he would have suspected that I was considering enlisting. I had the dream job for a young man just out of high school who was not going to college. However, the Armed Forces recruiting offices were in the basement of the post office, and that's why I was going there.

I don't remember thinking about enlisting in advance. I had dreamed about being a Navy officer, but I had had no other military aspirations. But I didn't want to stay at the mill and I had no way to pay for college. The only other option I could think of was enlisting.

I went down the stairs of the post office having absolutely no idea which branch I would join. (This has always been the way I do my Christmas shopping or birthday shopping. You know, I just go in the store and look around, hoping something will catch my eye.) Once I was there, I looked around. The Army recruiter was not in his office. The Navy recruiter was there; but my two older brothers had enlisted in the Navy. I wanted to be a Naval officer, but I did not want to wear one of the silly sailor uniforms of the Navy enlisted man: the ones with the Dixie cup hats and bell-bottom pants. Yuck! So, I would not join the Navy. I looked at the Air Force recruiter and a voice in my head told me that to be in the Air Force was to be no more than a civilian in uniform. If I was going to be in the military, I was not going to be a civilian. That left the Marine Corps. (Yes, this was how I chose the Marine Corps. It wasn't the reputation; it wasn't the awesome uniform; it wasn't anything else; it was simply the one that caught my eye.)

My sister Judy's husband Al – we knew him as "Herk", short I think for Hercules – was in the Marines; and my sister Francis' husband Dave had been a Marine mechanic on the Presidential helicopter. But I did not have this in mind at all. I simply decided, on the spot, I would join the Marine Corps because I didn't want to join the Navy or Air Force and the Army was not an option because the office was closed.

I approached the Marine recruiter. He rubbed his hands and smiled – I'm not sure about this, but that's how I remember it. I sat down. He said, "Let me tell you what the Marine Corps has to offer you." I stopped him. (I, who would soon be a Marine Corps maggot – our Drill Instructors' favorite name for us in boot camp – stopped a Marine Staff Sergeant.) I honestly do not know what I was thinking; but I told him, "No! I don't want you to lie to me. Just give me the papers and I will sign them." With only the slightest bit of hesitation, (and probably a wink at his fellow recruiter), the recruiter proceeded to place papers in front of me for me to

The Far-Away Dream

sign. In a flash I had enlisted in the Marine Corps. It was faster than filling out an application to work at McDonald's. (Believe me, I know, I had worked at McDonald's for a short time in high school.)

Now, remember, Mr. Ruby, who drove me to and from work, had dropped me off in Rochester on our way home. Home was still five miles away. When I finally arrived home – a couple of hours late, since I had spent some time with the recruiter and I had to hitch a ride for the second half of the trip home from the Rochester post office – my mother and father were sitting in the kitchen. I was afraid to talk to my dad about what I had done, so I asked my mother to join me in the living room. There I whispered to her that I had joined the Marine Corps. Dad, still in the kitchen, but only a short distance away, heard me, and he exploded. "You did what?"

From that moment until I left for boot camp a week or so later, my father refused to talk to me. On the morning my mother was going to drive me to catch a bus to Pittsburgh, I went into my parents' bedroom to say good-bye to Dad. He was in bed with his back to me. He just waved me off. He would not even say good-bye. But as it turned out, the first letter I received at Parris Island was from Dad. In it he explained that he had not talked to me because he was devastated by the fact that I had left a secure, draft-exempt job and had placed myself directly in harm's way. He had not turned around in bed to say good-bye because he was crying and I had never seen him cry. I had no idea until then how much my dad loved me. I still consider that the most wonderful letter I have ever received.

Soon my dad's words resounded in my ears, "You did what?" I had no idea what I had done. It was the summer of 1967. The war in Vietnam was heating up. Other recent graduates were being drafted so that they could be sent to the war. I had just started a job that rendered me draft exempt. And I had done what? My dad knew. My mother knew. But I did not. As far as I was concerned I was getting away from the heat and filth of the mill. I was oblivious to the heat and filth I would soon encounter, not to mention the heat and pressure of Parris Island, South Carolina. But of course, that's what came first: Marine Corps Recruit Depot, Parris Island, South Carolina. Although even that was preceded by one very embarrassing episode.

My mother dropped me off at a bus stop in Rochester. The bus took me to Pittsburgh, to the military induction center. The final phase of induction involved a physical examination. This was the day I was to travel to South Carolina. Strange as it may seem, the physical exam did not occur until this day. I guess if I had failed the exam, I would simply have been sent back home. There were quite a few of us undergoing the exam. We were standing naked except for our underwear. A football player named Roland, who I had just met that day, from Beaver High School – a school in my school's conference – called out for everyone to hear, "Hey Crum! I know the Marine Corps builds men; but you got to give them something to work with first." I was just shy of 6 feet tall and I weighed 125 lbs. The place erupted in laughter. Thanks, Roland, I needed that!

Boot Camp

Like all other Marine recruits, we arrived at the recruit depot at Parris Island, South Carolina, early in the dark hours of the morning. A drill instructor boarded the bus and yelled for us to quickly get off. Our lives were about to get disturbingly miserable.

Other than sleeping over at a cousin's house and sleeping outside on our porch or at Dave Wallace's tiny bunkhouse behind his home (we called it "the Sugar Shack"), I don't believe I ever spent a night away from my parents. I had not gone to summer camp. I had not vacationed away from my parents like my sister Frances and my brother Bill had done. I had spent one or two nights away at a Baptist teen conference in Erie with the Staffords. Other than that, I had not really been away from home and certainly not on my own. And here I was at Parris Island with some crazy men screaming at me, virtually non-stop for the first few weeks, or at least that's how it seemed. For the first 48 hours or so we were not permitted to go to bed. I was still in civilian clothes the second day at Parris Island white-washing some stones along a pathway and thinking, "What have I done? Where am I?"

Our platoon had around 60 men. We all slept in bunk beds in one long squad bay. Once training got underway, we got up each morning at 5 am (0500) and lights were out around 9 pm (2100). We would run first thing in the morning. This was by far my favorite time of the day. But the days were long and the drill instructors were relentless. I arrived at Parris Island on July 27th, which means I was there throughout the grueling month of August. It was hot; it was humid; and there were sand fleas everywhere. Sand fleas, we were told, were government property; and we were forbidden to destroy any government property – that meant we were not permitted to swat or squish any of the fleas.

Parris Island had a weather flag system to alert drill instructors to the weather conditions. A black flag indicated physical training was to be suspended. The drill instructors interpreted this to mean that physical training was to be done out of sight. Whenever there was a black flag, all physical training was done indoors in the squad bay in the barracks. Our barracks were old wooden structures with no air conditioning and very poor ventilation. During black flag periods, the wooden floor of our squad bay would become a pool from our perspiration. I never knew I could sweat so much. Of course, I also never knew I could endure so much. (One

The Far-Away Dream

night in Vietnam after a day of fierce combat, the men of my squad were sitting in a circle and someone asked the question, "Where would you rather be right now, here or at Parris Island?" No one said Parris Island. I would say the Marine Corps designed boot camp to get this response.)

A few days or a couple of weeks after arriving – I don't remember which – I was on duty as the first fire watch of the night. (Fire watch was divided into 8 1-hour segments each night. We were to make sure everyone stayed in their bunk and to keep watch for fire. In 1967 we were in World War II vintage wooden barracks, that could be consumed by a fire in minutes. It would not do for someone to light up a cigarette in bed.) The others had just hit the sack. The lights had been turned out and the duty DI (Drill Instructor) was in his room. One of the men – a hoodlum from Pittsburgh who had been given the option to go to jail or join the Marine Corps – had gotten out of his bunk, walked across from top bunk to top bunk until he found the person he was targeting, gave him a few crushing blows, and then began to return to his bunk. I called out his name. Immediately the drill instructor came into the squad bay. He asked me what was going on. I told him. He grabbed the thug, took him into the hallway and commenced to apply some old-fashioned Marine Corps discipline. Then he sent the battered offender back to bed. The next morning, I was relieving myself at the urinal, when this fellow recruit paid me a visit. I felt the force of his anger. Nothing like *esprit de corps*!

I happened to know that this man had been given the option of jail or the Marine Corps because he was one of twenty or so men who had gone through induction in Pittsburgh with me. When we were leaving the induction center for the airport I was handed a folder with all our orders and was told I was responsible for getting everyone to Parris Island. At the airport, this man and one other began drinking at a bar. I tried to get them to stop; that's when they informed me of their background and the option they had been given. They knew they had to go to Parris Island; but they were not going to go there sober.

On another occasion, we were going through the obstacle course with full combat gear. I looked out and saw Roland – you know, the football player from Beaver High? – he could not get over a wall that I had flown over. Although we were not permitted to speak unless spoken to, I yelled out to Roland, for everyone to hear, "Hey Roland, I know the Marine Corps builds men, but you got to give them something to work with first." The DIs dismissed my uninvited words and joined the others and laughed. (By the way, at the end of boot camp I weighed a whopping 150 lbs.)

After weeks of morning runs, close order drill (marching with rifles), hours in classrooms, physical fitness, physical fitness, physical fitness, and

The Far-Away Dream

harassment, harassment, harassment, recruit training finally came to an end. The day of our graduation, Gunnery Sergeant Glenn, our senior DI, was reading our orders and joking with us, something he had never done nor had any of the other DIs. When he came to my name and read that I was to be an 0311/rifleman and I was to go to the Republic of South Vietnam, he recalled that I had fired the lowest score on the rifle range and he quipped, "Hey Private Crum, when you get to Nam, find yourself a bow and arrow!" I laughed with the others and was happy that he would joke with me. (In Vietnam, I did something even better, I eventually found an M-79 grenade launcher and I became a grenadier.)

Throughout the 9 or 10 weeks of boot camp (shortened from 12 or 13 weeks because of the increased need for men in Vietnam) we had no opportunities for developing friendships. We were rarely permitted to talk to one another. But there are two men who stand out in my mind. (I know their names, but I won't say what they were.) One was a recruit from Rocky Mount, North Carolina. I remember him because the character Bubba in *Forest Gump* reminds me of him. He was just as big, just as black, and just as charming. I cannot imagine anyone not liking him. Even the drill instructors liked him. Well, maybe not Sergeant (Sgt.) Cargill. I'm not sure Sgt. Cargill ever liked anyone. My apologies to his family.

I also remember another man. This man's mother wrote a letter to the Marine Corps that Gunnery Sergeant (GySgt. or Gunny) Glenn shared with us. In it she said that she had signed for her son to enter the Corps although he was under age. Nevertheless, she was now withdrawing her permission and wanted the Marine Corps to release him and send him home. When this didn't work, she sent another letter. This one claimed that her son had been shot in the leg when he was young and the bullet had not been removed. She insisted that her boy should have failed his entrance physical exam and should now be granted a medical discharge. While this attempt also failed, GySgt. Glenn "appreciated" the concern this man's mother showed for her son and he took him under his wing. I think we all liked this man and the way Gunny Glenn took care of him.

Infantry Training and Guerilla Warfare Training

Boot camp was followed by Basic Infantry Training at Camp Geiger, Camp Lejeune, North Carolina. All Marines received this training, since all Marines are basically "grunts" or infantry. For those of us who were nothing but grunts (infantrymen), Basic Infantry Training was immediately followed by Advanced

Infantry Training. There were aspects of infantry training that were actually fun. Since I had been a long-distance runner in high school, I enjoyed most of the runs and even the long hikes. It was especially exciting to fire some of the wide variety of weapons, such as the Browning Automatic Rifle (BAR), the flame thrower, the machine gun and some of the mortars. We had occasional opportunities to fraternize during this phase of training. We even had some free time, although we could not leave Camp Geiger, our training camp. We never even saw the main base of Camp Lejeune. I do remember going to chapel each Sunday morning and singing in the choir. I am pretty sure this was the only time in my life that I ever sang in a church choir. I also recall going to dinner one day and discovering that the meal consisted of shrimp cocktail, prime rib, baked potatoes and cake. We found out it was the Marine Corps birthday and that this was the meal served that day in every Marine Corps mess hall. I have celebrated November 10th ever since.

I believe it is possible that I may have the record for holding the rank of E-1/Private the longest. It is true that I had the lowest score in my boot camp platoon on the rifle range; but I had no other blemishes on my record. I did very well in all the physical fitness tests, I had no problems with close order drill, and I could quickly answer any question I was asked. I suspect, however, that one of my infantry training troop handlers blocked my promotion to Private First Class (PFC) because I refused to laugh at his dirty jokes. It's not that I had never laughed at or even told dirty jokes. I had. But something else was occurring in me as I was being trained to be a combat Marine. I was also growing in my personal commitment as a Christian. I was praying more than I ever had in my life and I was much more concerned about how my life reflected my faith in Christ. I had no one to counsel me in this area of my life, I didn't give it a whole lot of thought; it was just something that was happening. And I think this prepared me for combat like nothing else could. Today I would say the Lord was preparing me for what I was soon to face.

Following infantry training I had a month of leave – from mid-November to mid-December. I spent this time at home in New Brighton. When it was time to leave, I was driven to the Pittsburgh airport by my mother and some of my sisters. Heavy snow slowed our drive to the airport. Mom dropped my sisters and me off while she went to park the car. Before she could join us, I had to board the plane. Mom and I did not get to say good-bye to each other. It was just as well that we didn't. It would have been an extremely difficult parting.

I was off to Camp Pendleton in California for Guerilla Warfare Training. (Camp Pendleton is on the Pacific coast between Los Angeles and San Diego.) I personally had orders to report to Monterrey Language

School, after my training at Camp Pendleton, to learn Vietnamese so that I could be a translator. But these orders were cancelled; most likely due to the increase in fighting in Vietnam and the need for more men immediately. So, I went to Vietnam as a rifleman and not as a translator.

While I was in training at Camp Pendleton, my Marine Corps brother-in-law, Herk, was stationed at Marine Corps Recruit Depot in San Diego, just a short bus ride south of Camp Pendleton. I could visit him, my sister Judy, and their two daughters, Diane and Mary, a few times before shipping out for Vietnam. I spent Christmas with them (and it snowed in San Diego that year – December 1967; you can look it up).

It was also during Guerilla Warfare Training that I met one of the best friends I had during my time in the Marine Corps. His name was Ed Iby. Ed was from South Philadelphia, from an Italian neighborhood. Ed's family was not Italian but he claimed his mother made the best lasagna in all South Philly. He introduced me to this Italian staple at a restaurant in Oceanside, California. To this day I regard that lasagna as the best I have ever eaten. With Ed I also had anchovies on pizza for the first and only time in my life. Ed warned me not to include them; but I wouldn't listen. Sometimes we just learn the hard way.

Ed and I spent a few more weeks in southern California than we should have. One afternoon, after our training had ended, we left our training unit to take a walk. While we were gone the unit had a roll-call formation. Because we missed this roll call we were removed from that unit and were replaced with other men. The next day that unit shipped out for Vietnam. We were assigned to various work details, such as cleaning offices and acting as couriers, carrying memos from one office to another (I guess that's how it was done before the internet). It was two weeks before we were assigned to another unit and shipped out. This "discipline" resulted in two more weekends of off-base liberty and allowed us to watch the Super Bowl in January 1968 in the comfort of Southern California. Perhaps we should have gone for some more walks.

From Home to Vietnam: Travis Air Force Base and Okinawa

Finally, we were on our way. We boarded busses and were taken to Travis Air Force Base, our departure point from "the world". At Travis we ate at the enlisted "dining hall". In six months as a Marine, I had never eaten at a dining hall. All our meals – with the exception for those that were eaten in the field – had been eaten in chow halls or mess halls. For the first time we ate in a "dining" hall. Also for the first time we had our drinks in glasses not hard plastic cups, and our food was on ceramic plates not on metal trays or hard plastic plates. This was like the last meal of a condemned convict who was about to be executed. We found it hard to believe that they would trust us with such finery. Honestly, we were tempted to throw the glasses, just to prove we were not truly capable of handling such fragile objects.

From Travis, we flew to Okinawa. I believe all Marines went to Okinawa on their way to Vietnam and on their way home from Vietnam. But being a PFC (Private First Class, finally), I did not know this was our itinerary. I thought we were going straight to Vietnam. So, when our busses took us from the airport to Camp Butler, I thought we were already in Vietnam. I looked out the window and saw only Asian people. I was sure they were Vietnamese. I couldn't believe it. Where was my rifle? (Even if I was a lousy shot, I would feel better with a rifle than without one.) What if we were attacked? When someone noticed my "discomfort", I was told this was not Vietnam but a place called Okinawa. Yes, I was that ignorant and that naïve.

We spent about a week on Okinawa getting our final round of inoculations and storing a sea bag with those items we would not need in Vietnam. Then it was time to go. I should have been at St. Joe Lead. Instead I was headed for Danang.

David A. Crum

From Home to Vietnam: a cook and a true friend

On the flight to Danang from Okinawa I was seated next to a Marine who told me he was a cook. When I told him I was an 0311/rifleman. He extended his hand to shake mine and said, "It's been nice knowing ya!" Then he quoted what he had heard was the life expectancy of a grunt. How I wished I had my rifle. Even I couldn't miss from this range. I wondered how one Marine could say such a thing to another Marine. So much for Marine cooks. (I bet he was surprised a few weeks later when truck drivers, clerks and cooks were sent to the front line to fight alongside 0311 grunts during the Tet Offensive.)

Once we arrived in South Vietnam we spent a night in a barracks at the Danang airfield. The next day we awaited flights to the places where we would join the units to which we were being assigned. Ed Iby and I waited together at the terminal. My flight came before his. We smiled and said our good-byes. A year later we met on Okinawa again when Ed was on his way home. He told me then that as soon as I left the Danang terminal to board my plane, he began to cry. He was afraid I would die. I was a grunt. He was an air traffic controller. He knew the statistics the cook had quoted; but he kept them to himself. That's what I would expect from a Marine. That's what I got from a friend. He

The Far-Away Dream

said nothing, smiled, waited till I left, then he cried. (As an aside: Ed Iby served his 13-month tour of duty in Vietnam without suffering any injuries, although he did endure a bout of malaria. However, during his one month of leave upon returning home, he sustained a broken collar bone in a car accident. He recovered from his injury and completed his enlistment; but we both were left to wonder if we had survived Vietnam only to be killed on the highway.)

Marine Squad on the Attack by Ben Crum

Chapter Three

Vietnam

Jesus said, *"If anyone wishes to come after Me, he must deny himself, and take up his cross and follow Me. For whoever wishes to save his life will lose it, but whoever loses his life for My sake and the gospel's will save it."*

— Mark 8:34-35

Jesus also said, *"Greater love has no one than this, that one lay down his life for his friends."*

— John 15:13

Phu Bai and Hotel, 2/5

I never thought about dying. Just like the day I enlisted, the question could be asked, "What on earth was I thinking?" I don't know. I only know I was not thinking of death or even of being injured. I boarded the plane and I was on my way to Phu Bai, the base camp of the 2nd Battalion, Fifth Marine Regiment, of the First Marine Division. I would report to Hotel Company – Hotel, 2/5.

I had only flown a few times in my life. My first flight was from Pittsburgh to North Carolina on my way to Parris Island. My second flight was back home to Pittsburgh. My third was to Southern California on my way to Camp Pendleton. My fourth was to Okinawa. My fifth was to Danang. This was my sixth flight – the flight from Danang to Phu Bai. I have flown many times since; but this flight was one of a kind. It was a prop plane that had been stripped inside. I think there were seats and seatbelts, but not much else. There was no insulation and it was noisy. It was also rocky. And I think we were being fired at. All I know is I was really glad to get off that plane.

I spent a couple of nights at Phu Bai sleeping on a cot in a large tent. We could hear shooting and mortar fire. Another new man and I ran out of the tent to a nearby bunker the first time this happened. The old salts laughed at us and told us the fight was a long way off.

Our second night at Phu Bai we watched Raquel Welch in the movie "1 Million Years B.C". It was being shown outside, using a sheet as a screen. During the movie we could hear shooting. I have never been so uncomfortable watching a movie (except perhaps watching Mel Brook's "Blazing Saddles" at a theater in Lakeland, Florida, with my new wife and my parents). The next night we watched a couple of episodes of a TV show called, of all things, "Combat." The other new man and I were looking for cover every time gunfire erupted on screen. Whoever made the decision to "entertain" us with "Combat" episodes must have had a sick sense of humor.

I don't remember their names

After a couple of days in Phu Bai, I was taken to the site where my unit was encamped. It was along the main road between Danang and Phu Bai. I think it was called U.S. 1. (Being only a PFC there was much I didn't know and very little that I did know.) I was assigned to the first squad of the first platoon and was taken over to meet the men.

[I regret to say that I have a complete mental block when it comes to the names of these men. This is quite surprising to me since I have always been good with names. I only remember the names of the company Gunnery Sergeant, Frank Thomas; my first platoon commander, 2nd Lieutenant Myers; the company commander, Captain Ron Christmas; and the first name of our Corpsman – Dennis. Years later, when I reported as a chaplain to the 1st Marine Division, I was being introduced to the Commanding General. When I told him, I had fought with the 2nd Battalion, 5th Marines in Hue, he asked me if I knew the name of my battalion commander. I told him that I did not. He asked me if I knew the name of my company commander. I responded, yes, that his name was Captain Ron Christmas. (Officers' ranks are part of their names as far as I am concerned.) The general asked me again if I knew the name of my battalion commander. I replied that I had only been a PFC, that I had never met the battalion commander, and that I did not know his name. With a smile the general told me, "I was your battalion commander." His name was Ernie Cheatham. His rise to the command of the 1st Marine Division was, no doubt, largely due to his command of the 2nd Battalion, 5th Marines during the Battle of Hue. I should have known this. Now that was embarrassing.]

The men in the squad welcomed me kindly. The first man offered me a cigarette. I said, "No thanks, I don't smoke." The second man offered me a cup of coffee. I said, "No thanks, I don't drink coffee." Someone declared, "I'll give you two weeks. You'll be drinking coffee and smoking." I wish I could have accepted their hospitality. I soon learned that the men depended on coffee and cigarettes to relax. As it turned out, I did not need those, I had prayer and through prayer access to the One who kept me as relaxed as I could possibly be. It has been 50 years and I am still not smoking and I don't drink coffee. However, to this day I appreciate the warm welcome those men gave me and how they drew me into the platoon, the squad, and my first fire team.

Preparing for combat

In high school, I had read *The Red Badge of Courage* by Stephen Crane. It is a story of a young man, actually a teenager, who had lied about his age to enlist in the Union army during the Civil War (or, as my Southern friends have told me, the War of Northern Aggression). As the time comes when this very young soldier is about to enter combat for the first time, he wonders what he will do. Will he stand and fight or will he run and hide? This thought occurred to me while I was on my way to Vietnam, but I don't remember thinking it once I was there. I was now part of an actual combat unit, and I would do whatever we were ordered to do.

For the first week or so, we would go out on patrols at night, not too far from our base camp, and set up positions in the thick growth of trees and bushes. I don't really know what the object was – no one ever told me and I never asked. I think we were providing perimeter protection for the base camp as well as scouting any enemy movement. We did not engage the enemy at all during this time. We did, however, encounter many annoying insects. We wore an insect repellant that was odorless and quite effective. (It was critical that the repellant was odorless. Some sweet-smelling repellant would have given away our presence.) We called the repellent "bug juice". The bugs were buzzing all around us. We let them be. (No pun intended!) Who would have thought that being punished by drill instructors for slapping sand fleas at Parris Island would teach us a discipline that could save our lives?

The Tet offensive begins

One night, at the very end of January, our entire platoon was told to "saddle up" – gather all our gear and prepare to move out. We headed north on the road next to which our camp had been located. (I believe we were providing ongoing security for travel on this road.) We walked on the road with one man on the right side and the next man on the left side of the road for as long as the number of men in the platoon stretched. We kept plenty of space between each man. (I had no idea that on this night the North Vietnamese army and the Vietcong were launching the 1968 Tet Offensive. We were on our way to protect some bridges that were a few miles north of our position.) This was the night my combat experience truly began.

The road we were on had steep embankments on either side. I was on the left side of the road. All of a sudden, we were being fired on. We were ordered to take cover. We moved off the road, down the embankment.

Soon I realized everyone else had taken cover down the embankment on the right side of the road. I had gone down the nearest embankment, the one to my left. The problem was we were being fired on from the left flank. When I noticed I was alone on the left side of the road, I immediately got up and ran across to the other, safer side, joining the rest of the platoon. So much for my first taste of combat.

I don't know how it was decided that it was safe to get back on the road, but before long we were on the road again, moving now at a much quicker pace. We reached the first bridge while it was still dark. The bridge had been attacked. The Marines there had sustained some casualties, but they had successfully protected the bridge. As soon as there was any morning light, we were sent off the road into a rice paddy and a bordering wood in pursuit of those who had attacked the bridge. My squad was the point squad. I was somewhere near the front.

Witnessing death

We were just outside the wooded area (an area with lots of trees and heavy brush, yet not a forest or jungle). We were about to enter it, when the enemy opened fire on us. A man right in front of me was shot and killed. This man was not in my team. But he was the first man I saw killed. He may have been from another squad. I know nothing about him. I only know I saw him get shot and he was immediately dead.

We returned fire until it was clear we were no longer being fired upon. Since I was near the front just behind the man who had been shot, it was determined that I must know where the enemy was. I was told to take off all my extra gear – my gas mask, my back pack, extra ammunition, and a few other items. Then I was sent into the wood. There was a dry creek bed. I was ordered to crawl in the creek bed until I located the enemy. What can I say, I did what I was told to do, although I once again had no idea what was being expected of me. (As I think about this now, I wonder how often individuals and small units are sent into situations like this. They have no idea what is expected of them. Those sending them may not even have a clear plan. But something must be done, and so, someone in authority decides to give an order. And those who are given the order simply do what they are told to do. This is part of what is involved in being under authority.)

I must have crawled fifty feet or so, when I heard a thump. The thump was followed by an explosion. The enemy had seen me before I had seen them and had tossed a grenade at me. I was not hit. I did not even bother to turn around. I simply crawled out of the creek bed and out of the wood, back to my platoon, backwards. (I know this may sound like a comedy, but believe me, I wasn't laughing.)

The Far-Away Dream

    Once I reached my platoon, now they were convinced I knew where the enemy was. My squad leader was ordered to take our squad around the right flank, with me at point, to come on the other side of the enemy. Off we went. There were woods here, so I led the squad being careful to stay inside the tree line. When we reached a certain spot, I told the squad leader that I thought we were close to the enemy position. He ordered us to each take a grenade, pull out the pin, then throw it on his command.

    (You can pull the pin on a grenade and hold it in your hand without worrying about it exploding. The pin is through a handle. You could put the pin back into the handle then safely place the grenade back on your belt or in a pack, wherever you carry your grenades, without it going off. But once the handle comes off the grenade then it will explode in a matter of seconds.)

    When we were ready, the squad leader gave the command for us to throw our grenades. We all threw our grenades. Suddenly, my team leader, my best friend at the time, yelled that his grenade had slipped out of his hand. We all dove for cover. All the grenades exploded with my team leader's grenade exploding just a few yards in front of us. No one was hit. However, the squad leader – who happened to be my team leader's best friend – shouted at him in anger and frustration, telling him to take the point. Without thinking, my team leader stepped out of the woods into a clearing. I prepared to follow him.

Before I was entirely on my feet, a machine gun opened fire. I watched as my team leader was picked up off his feet, being lifted in the air by the power and volume of the rounds that were hitting him. The enemy had survived our volley of grenades. They were where I thought they were, and now they knew exactly where we were. For the second time that day, a man – this time my best friend – died just a few feet in front of me. We took cover.

Gunnery Sergeant Frank Thomas

The next thing that happened was one of the craziest and bravest things I have ever seen.

The company gunnery sergeant, Frank Thomas, made his way over to our squad. When he saw my team leader lying out in the open, he was not going to allow the enemy to continue filling him with holes and throwing grenades at him – something they had been doing since the time they had first shot him. GySgt. Thomas ran out, picked him up, and carried him back to where we had taken cover. We wrapped the body in my poncho liner and carried him back to the rest of the platoon. This was the first time I witnessed the selfless bravery of Gunny Thomas. It would not be the last.

The Far-Away Dream

On line through the woods

Then we did something that you don't hear of every day in connection with the war in Vietnam. We got on line – the whole platoon – and walked through the woods, firing as we moved. No fire was returned. The enemy was on the run. We walked right through the place they had occupied.

This ended that first day of the Tet Offensive; except I remember when we got back to the road, near the bridge, there were some bodies of dead Vietcong lying on the side of the road. I went over to one of the bodies, kneeled beside it and examined it closely. I wanted to look at death and see how I would react. The body looked like a busted mannequin. I was not sick. I was not shocked or repulsed. I was fine. I got up and joined my squad. I was convinced I could handle the death that accompanied combat. Just then a member of my team, who was from Chicago, knowing I had considered our team leader my best friend, came over to me and told me he would now be my best friend; another wonderful gesture. This man died less than two weeks later in the city of Hue (pronounced "way").

That evening we were back next to the road again, digging fox holes. We could hear fighting all around us, near and far. So, I thought, this is what a major battle sounds like in person. (No wonder some combat veterans have such a difficult time enjoying fireworks on the 4th of July.) In the morning, we boarded trucks and were driven to Phu Bai. After a day or so in Phu Bai, we were on trucks again heading to the city of Hue.

On the road from Phu Bai to Hue we took incoming fire on at least three occasions. Each time we had to disembark the trucks and set up defensive positions. (Of all the infantry training we had received, I don't remember being trained in how to quickly disembark and then climb back onto trucks. This was definitely on-the-job training. We did some major scrambling getting off those trucks, then climbing back on again.) As far as I know the only injuries we encountered on the road occurred when a truck rolled back on a few of the men who were positioned behind it.

The Battle of Hue

Of course, the vast majority of us had no idea where we were headed. When we pulled onto the streets of Hue we couldn't believe our eyes. We had all grown up watching movies of World War II, including the previously mentioned TV series "Combat". It felt like we were in one of those movies. The streets were littered with trucks and tanks that had been blown up. When we jumped down onto the pavement, I remember looking at the trucks and tanks, examining my own flak jacket and helmet, and wondering something like, "Whoa, we're in trouble!" One of the training exercises in infantry training was learning how to fight in an urban setting. There was a mock town called "combat town". For one of the few times in the Vietnam War, fighting would take place in a combat town, better known as the city of Hue.

My platoon made its way to one of the buildings of the University of Hue. We were there for some time – I believe for three or more days. A number of men were shot during that time. I remember being alone in a library. (I found a book of poems in English by Elizabeth Barrett Browning. I tore out one page. The poem on that page began, "How do I love thee? Let me count the ways." I had heard that poem in high school. I know the author was writing about her love for a man; but I read in these words my love for my Lord. I placed the page in my Bible.) While in the library a thought entered my mind, "We're all gonna die." This thought was followed instantly by another thought, "But not me." Still, with men dying all around me, I did not think I would die. (In the years that have followed that day in the Hue University library, I have wondered if my having these two rapid thoughts was a way of the Lord reassuring me that, because of my faith in Jesus Christ, even if I would die I would have life in Him – eternal life. I have come to believe that the reason I was not afraid of dying, why I did not even think of dying, was because God had so convinced me that I would live even if I had died.)

I was not privy to any of the discussions our leaders were having, all I know is that after a few days of fighting from within the confines of that university building, we were told to get ready. We were to put on our gas masks and to line up at one of the exit doors. We were about to commence fighting – house to house, street by street. I was either the second or the third man out the door. We were to run across a street into a building on the other side.

Infantry Training: "Combat Town"

This is where my "take everything seriously" approach to life was of great benefit to me. When we were being instructed on urban warfare in infantry training, I remember a number of the men complaining that this was a waste of time, since we would be fighting in the rice paddies and jungles of Vietnam, not in any cities. On the other hand, I felt that if the Marine Corps decided we needed to learn how to fight in cities, then I should learn all I could about how to fight in cities. I remember going through "combat town" with great enthusiasm and with the intention of doing what I was being trained to do. At one point I was on the second floor of a building where the window of the adjacent building was four feet or so from a window in my building. We had been taught that if you can move from one building to another without going down to ground level, you should do it. I proceeded to dive through the window in my building and through the window in the other building (there was no glass in the windows). I rolled up onto my feet and an instructor, who was in the room I had entered, threw me against a wall. I bounced off the wall and shot him (without any rounds in my rifle of course). The instructor shouted, "That's the way it's done!" I also learned to always assume the enemy was waiting for me in any building I would enter. In Hue, I always threw a grenade into a building before entering, then I entered firing my rifle.

Hue: On point

As I said, when we left the university building and headed for the building across the street, I was either the second or third man out the door. By the time we reached the building, I was the first man through the door. From then on, I was on point. I would be the first man as we moved from building to building. We did this for a couple of days. On the second or third day we came to a string of houses that had high concrete walls around them. I was about to go through a hole in one of these walls when a shot rang out and a round struck the inside of the wall right next to my head. We were able to determine, after another try, that a sniper was zeroed in on that hole in the wall. (Fortunately for me, the sniper was not an expert sniper.)

Many of the buildings in this part of town had some sort of crawl space between the roof and the ceiling on the top floor. It was not uncommon for snipers to use this space for their vantage point. We were sure that was what a sniper was doing now. A call went in for an Ontos to be brought up to remove the sniper. (An Ontos was an anti-tank vehicle armed with recoilless rifles.) We sat down on our side of the wall, waiting for the sniper threat to be removed. This was a welcomed rest.

Wounded for the first time

I had been saving some sugar and powdered milk for the right time, so that I could mix them with some hot chocolate and make some sweet and creamy cocoa. I mixed the ingredients with some water in my canteen cup, lit some C-4 under it, and in less than a minute was ready to enjoy my long-waited treat. I took one sip and, to my great disappointment, discovered that I had accidentally added a package of coffee. I have no idea why I had a package of coffee in my pocket; but it was an easy mistake since the coffee and cream packages were about the same size. I do not drink coffee. I have never drunk coffee. I have tasted it and I know that I don't like it. I was in the process of tossing my tainted cocoa away when, to my surprise, the Ontos – now directly on the other side of the wall from where I was sitting – fired at the sniper position. (I wasn't even aware that the Ontos had arrived.) When the recoilless rifle fired, it sent sparks from a back blast over the wall.

Blast! by William Crum

Some sparks went down my back inside my flak jacket. I instinctively reached with my left arm and began to rub out the sparks with my left hand. Just as I did a rocket was fired by the enemy at the Ontos. The Ontos was hit and shrapnel came over the wall. Some of that shrapnel hit me. I sustained shrapnel wounds in my left arm pit and in my buttocks. My helmet and flak jacket must have prevented other shrapnel from hitting me in the head and in my side or chest.

I was immediately attended to by our corpsman.

A picture of him attending to me has been in many publications. I think it first appeared in a military publication, either "The Navy Times" or "Stars and Stripes". A couple of years later, my high school friend, Steve Murphy, saw the picture in *Time* magazine and told me about it. It accompanied an article on some sort of advanced medical training for former military corpsmen and medics. The corpsman who had attended to me was in that training, following his discharge from the Navy. Years later a fellow Navy chaplain gave me a book entitled *The Battle of Hue* that included the picture, and more recently it has graced the cover of *The Encyclopedia of Warfare*.

It has become the practice of members of our family to look for the picture. My son Nathaniel discovered it in a music video, "The 8th of November," by the country duo Big & Rich. Nate, serving in the Air Force at the time, was eating at a restaurant when the video was on a

*Corpsman D. R. Howe attending to PFC
David A. Crum*, National Archive

screen. The song is about a man who annually observes the 8th of November as the day on which a soldier in his Army unit performed an act of bravery that resulted in his being awarded the Medal of Honor. As the video progresses, there is a rapid succession of combat slides. Nate decided he would pay close attention, looking for my picture; and, sure enough, it appeared.

My sons, David and Thomas, both enlisted in the Marine Corps at the same time in 2009 and went through boot camp in the same series at Parris Island, although they were not in the same platoon. A few months out of boot camp, David was at Camp Lejeune in North Carolina and Thomas was at 29 Palms in California. Each one had gone to the base exchange on their respective bases and encountered the same thing. There was a display of the latest film on Vietnam, entitled "Goodbye Vietnam". That picture of me being attended to by the corpsman was on the cover of the video, and this time I am identified by name on the back of the jacket, as is the corpsman. His name is D. R. Howe. I knew him simply as Dennis.

The Battalion Aid Station (BAS)

Once the corpsman had examined me, I was taken to the Battalion Aid Station. There I received an examination and a shot. I could have been sent back to my platoon, except for the fact that I had no trousers.

(The corpsman had removed my flak jacket and shirt and also had ripped my trousers off to examine my buttocks wound). I had to wait at least two days until I was given a pair of trousers.

The medical staff and some of the Marines at the BAS were quite excited about what they found in the basement of the house where the aid station had been established. The French had been in Hue during the French-Indo-China War and some of the houses in this sector of Hue had some very impressive wine cellars. This was one of those houses. I enjoyed some of that wine – purely for medicinal purposes. No wonder I wasn't feeling much pain.

Of course during the time I was in the BAS many casualties were brought in for medical attention. There was one Marine who was brought in three times in those two days with three different wounds. After the first two times he was sent back out to fight. The third time he was placed on a helicopter. He was still walking. His wounds were not too serious. But with the "3-wounds-and-you're-out" policy, he was being removed from combat since he had been wounded on 3 separate occasions. I remain amazed that the Marine Corps would adhere so strictly to that policy. I don't know that it always did; but it did this time. I witnessed it. (Unless there was something else wrong with the man that I did not know about. Based on my range of knowledge, this is quite possible.)

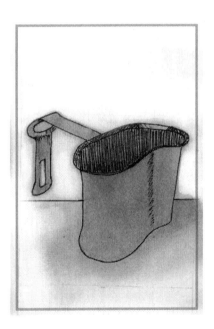

Wine from a Tin Cup by Jill Crum

Back in the fight

Finally, I was given a pair of trousers (as usual, I have no idea where they came from; I'll leave that to your imagination) and I was sent back to my platoon with my left arm in a sling. Lt. Myers was very pleased to have me back. The first obstacle we faced as we moved out was a wall he wanted us to climb over. Off came the sling, and over the wall I went. He placed me back on point. My team was ready to enter a building. I threw a grenade inside, then we went in, running from one end to the other, shooting our rifles as we went. When we reached the end of a long corridor, I turned around. Lt. Myers was holding two prisoners, one in each hand. He smiled at me and said, "Hey Crum, look what you missed." Our firing had kept them on the floor, out of sight. We may have missed them, but they had not been able to return our fire.

For the next few days we continued to fight through our sector of the city. One night we were lying in a courtyard. We did our best not to give away our position. There were rats in that courtyard; some were running around and over us. We remained still. The discipline of recruit training was evident in how we could cope with extremely difficult and uncomfortable circumstances. If nothing else, we were disciplined; not very comfortable, but disciplined.

What stands out in my mind about the fighting in Hue is the number of times I heard bullets whizzing by my head. (If you have seen the movie, "Saving Private Ryan," think about the scene of the beach landing and the sound of bullets all around the men. This captures that sound perfectly.) No wonder there were so many fatalities and casualties in Hue. A few inches left or right, front or back, could prove fatal. It is remarkable that we were not all killed. Any of us could have been killed on numerous occasions. Life and death was often a matter of feet or inches. As a matter of fact, after I had been wounded by the shrapnel from the rocket fired at the Ontos and had been taken off to the Battalion Aid Station, my platoon was able to continue on through the hole in the wall where I had been halted by the sniper. According to an account in *The Battle of Hue*, the first two men who entered the next building were killed. I would have been the first man in that building. Until I was injured, I was the point.

[While I attribute the fact that I was not killed to the grace of God, I in no way think I deserved to be spared and those who died deserved to die. God preserved me according to His own secret plan for my life. He would still be the same loving, sovereign God if He had not spared my life. The year I returned home from Vietnam my cousin Skip, who was also a Marine, was sent there. He spent much more time in combat than I had, attaining the rank of Corporal by the time he had been in the Corps for less than two years. He was as serious about his faith in Christ as I was, yet his life ended while mine was spared.

"On behalf of the President of the United States and a grateful nation" I presented the U. S. flag to his mother. Skip's name, Donald James Pierce, Jr. is on the Memorial Wall at the Vietnam Veterans' War Memorial in Washington, D.C. But Skip himself, due to his faith in Christ, is with our loving Lord.]

"Happy 19th Birthday!": Wounded a second time

On February 11th, we left the sector of Hue we had been fighting in and crossed a bridge over a canal. I remember the date well because it was my 19th birthday. I believe Hotel Company was the first unit on that side of the canal during the battle. My platoon led the company. My squad led the platoon. I was not the point; but my team was near the front.

The area had been recently occupied. We came upon smoking fire pits and even a freshly slaughtered pig. After patrolling near the canal all day, we set up inside a walled compound in the evening. We were given time to eat and rest. I was glad for the opportunity. I was able to get a can of pound cake in my C-rations and I had been saving a can of peaches. I was ready to celebrate my birthday in style.

As I was enjoying this birthday treat, not to mention a much-needed rest, my new team leader came over to tell me that the lieutenant was looking for some volunteers to go out on a listening post. I told him, "I hope you find some." He said, smiling at me, "I just found one." I told him this was my birthday. He said, "Happy Birthday, Crum!", without changing his mind about my being one of the "volunteers". He found one other "volunteer". Then the three of us – this other volunteer, the team leader and I – were sent out a hundred yards or so from the rest of the platoon. We had no radio. We were just to listen for movement; and, if we heard any, we were to come back and report it to the lieutenant. Off we went.

I have already mentioned that I do not remember the names of the men I fought with, except for a few of them. While I don't understand why this is so for all these men, I do understand why I do not remember the name of the other "volunteer" in this night's listening post. This man had reported to our platoon earlier that day, before we crossed the canal. This was his first and, most likely, his last day in combat.

We made our way in the dark a good distance from the platoon. My team leader motioned for us to kneel down. We were not there long, before we heard movement. As far as I was concerned, it was time to leave and report back to the platoon. The team leader wanted to stay. Before long a grenade was thrown at us and landed far enough away that none of us was injured. I heard where it came from and I quickly threw a grenade there. (Wasn't it time to leave now? What was my team leader waiting for? The whole platoon could hear what was going on.) The team leader pulled a pin on a grenade and held it in his hand. I immediately thought we are in big trouble if he is shot and he drops that grenade. I gave him a push and told him to throw the grenade. He did; and just as he did, I saw a flash of light on our left flank. In a moment the other man in our position let out a scream. He had been hit in his shoulder. I turned toward him and realized I had also been shot. For some reason I did not feel the bullets hit me, but as I turned I felt burning in my right ankle and my left thigh. It could be that that was the moment I was shot. However, the other man's reaction coincided with the flash of light, mine did not. At any rate, I had been shot in both my legs.

My first thought was, "I can't move." My second thought was, "Who's going to come and get me?" My third thought was, "Let's go!!!" These thoughts all occurred in a millisecond. At once I grabbed the other man and we were up, along with the team leader, running back to the platoon.

We arrived at Lieutenant Myers' position inside a house. He had the corpsman examine us. The corpsman took off my right boot; then, when he saw there was nothing he could do, he told me to put it back on. Putting that boot back on may have been the most painful thing I have ever done. Lt. Myers wanted us to go to the company headquarters. I had run from our listening post position back to the platoon on adrenaline. Now I could not even walk. Someone helped me get to the company command post. This was inside another house, a few blocks away. The two of us, the man with the shoulder injury and I, entered a room with Captain Ron Christmas, the company commander, and Gunnery Sergeant Frank Thomas, the company gunnery sergeant. They asked me about what had happened. They discussed the situation with each other. Then it was decided we needed to be taken back across the canal, since the Battalion Aid Station (BAS) was still there.

During all this time I do not remember this other Marine – the one who had been shot in his shoulder – ever saying anything. I believe he was in great pain and in shock. Though I had been shot in both my legs – one shot had gone through my left thigh, the other had gone through my right ankle – neither had hit any bone. This other man had been shot in the shoulder. His shoulder could have been shattered. How painful that must have been. This man did not throw a grenade and he never fired his rifle. If this wound was as serious as I think it

Gunny Thomas Crosses Back by Nate Crum

was, this was his first and last day in combat. Such is the possibility in a combat zone.

Gunnery Sergeant Frank Thomas again

We were faced with a few major obstacles. This other man was in great pain, I could not walk on my own, and we had to cross over the canal on a bridge that would make us an easy target. Gunnery Sergeant Thomas told Captain Christmas he would take us over the bridge. I doubt if Gunny Thomas was awarded any medal for this action; but what a tremendous act of bravery and selflessness. He took us over that bridge, helping both of us. A jeep was waiting for us on the other side to take us to the BAS. Gunny Thomas crossed back over the bridge and returned to the company CP (command post).

The ride in the jeep to the BAS was not long, but it was bumpy and thus very painful. The streets were worse than the streets of Philadelphia after a cold winter; even worse than the streets of Haiti – if that's possible. Once we arrived at the BAS the doctor examined us. The first thing I did was apologize to the doctor for being wounded again and troubling him. He just laughed and declared, "You Marines are so crazy!" The next day we were medevac'd by helicopter to Phu Bai.

At the Phu Bai field hospital

The first day at the Phu Bai hospital corpsmen came around the ward cleaning wounds. When a corpsman began to clean my wounds, he discovered that the wound in my right ankle had not been treated properly in surgery. I was sent back to the surgical room. There I saw other men from my platoon undergoing surgery. They had taken either mortar or artillery fire during the night after I had left. On the table next to me was Lt. Myers. I could hardly recognize him. His wounds were serious and extensive.

Putting my boot back on my foot after the corpsman had removed it may have been the most painful experience I have ever had; but close behind that was the regular cleaning of my wounds at the field hospital in Phu Bai. It got to the point that I began sweating profusely in anticipation of their cleaning as the corpsmen who were making the rounds approached me. I will spare you the details.

Seventeen years later, in 1985, I was serving as a Navy Chaplain with the 2nd Battalion, 7th Marine Regiment. We were on Okinawa. Our battalion Sergeant Major had a visitor he wanted me to see in his office. The visitor was the Sergeant Major of the Third Marine Division. It was Frank Thomas. Sgt. Major Thomas and I spoke for a while that day and met on one or two other occasions. He told me about the success he and

Captain Christmas had had. Captain Christmas was either a Colonel or a Brigadier General by this time. He retired as a Lieutenant General. Sgt. Major Thomas also told me about Lt. Myers. His wounds the night of February 11-12 were career ending. The last time I spoke with him was when I had been shot in both my legs. The last time I saw him was when he was lying on the surgical table.

Phu Bai: Other kinds of combat

I was in the field hospital at Phu Bai for a week or so. Finally, I was released; but I had to remain in Phu Bai until my stitches were removed and I was declared physically fit to return to combat. I spent daylight hours at or near the chapel. I especially remember one young Marine I met there. (If I considered him young, he must have been eighteen, while I was an elderly nineteen, plus a week or so.) This other Marine was in Phu Bai because he had lost his night vision. He simply could not see once it was dark. I spoke to him about the deep faith I had in Jesus Christ. We talked about this for a number of days. We read the Bible, talked about what it said, and often prayed together. A few weeks later, after I had returned to Hue, I received a letter from him. He told me he had asked the chaplain to baptize him. He was anxious to tell his mother. She had wanted him to come to faith in Christ and to get baptized for years.

She had been praying for him. God used this time in Vietnam to bring her son to Christ and to give him the assurance of eternal life.

I was really anxious to leave Phu Bai and to return to my unit. From time to time Phu Bai was the target of incoming artillery, and I felt much more comfortable being fired upon by an enemy that I could fire back at. For example, one day we were eating lunch in the mess hall when we began to hear incoming artillery rounds. We picked up our trays and hustled into some bunkers. We had just arrived at the bunker when we heard an explosion. We turned around and saw that the mess hall had taken a direct hit and had been destroyed. The next day I was on a truck heading back to Hue.

Back in Hue

I had missed the final two weeks of heavy fighting in Hue. Once I returned the battle was all but over. I returned to a much different platoon. During the month-long battle all but one man in my platoon had either been killed or wounded. [A platoon has over 40 men and our platoon was constantly being sent replacements when men were killed or injured. And so, it could have been that out of as many as 50 or 60 men, this one man was the only member of our platoon who was not killed or wounded during the month-long Battle of Hue; and a good number of us had been wounded more than once.]

I remember standing next to the one man who had not been injured saying I wanted to keep close to him for safety. He replied that he did not want to be anywhere near me for the same reason – for his own safety. Of my original fire team of four men, I was the only one still alive.

Finally, the battle was over. We knew it was over because the Army rolled into town on trucks and took over our positions so that we could track down the Vietcong (VC) and the North Vietnamese Army (NVA) on the outskirts of Hue.

The arrival of the Army unit was one of the worst episodes of my life. We were sitting in our posts next to a bridge. Soldiers on the trucks were making fun of us and throwing soap and candy bars – not any good ones, but the ones that came in C-rations that we referred to as "shit" bars. This was clearly not a gesture of good will. They were mocking us. We were dirty and our uniforms were quite shabby. They were clean and their uniforms looked fresh. They were well-fed and groomed. We were hungry and haggard. We had just fought a major battle. Many of our friends had either been killed or wounded (including Lt. Myers). We were mad! Personally, I have disliked the Army ever since.

Well, at any rate the Army took over our ***secure*** positions and we headed out into the surrounding farms and rice paddies. I don't think we would have had it any other way. After all, we were Marines.

After Hue

I was recovering from being shot in my left thigh and my right ankle. Sitting around in a bunker in Hue wasn't too bad. Hiking for miles each day in fields and rice paddies was another thing. The first day, after leaving Hue, we came upon some sort of boarding school. There was an outside basketball court. There was no basketball, but we created one out of some rags. Basketball was my favorite sport. I thought this would be a good way to test my legs to see how well I could jump and maneuver. I did not do very well. But what can I say? For one time in my life I simply bore the pain and went wherever the platoon went and did whatever the platoon did. I guess this is one of the reasons wars are often fought by young men – we healed quickly. Within a few days the pain was gone.

This was the beginning of my last two months in Vietnam. Although the regular tour of duty during the Vietnam War was 13 months, there was the policy that the tour of duty ended when a person was wounded three times. I would be wounded a third time in either late April or early May.

David A. Crum

"I Wish It Would Rain"

I don't believe our initial pursuit of the VC and NVA resulted in any sizable encounters. Occasionally we would come across a tunnel and one of us would go down into it to see what we could find. One time I came out with a transistor radio and a writing tablet. I put the paper to good use for the next couple of weeks, writing letters home; although it was a little awkward, since I had to write around a hole in the middle of each page. You see, before going down into that hole I had thrown a grenade. Shrapnel from the grenade had gone through the tablet, creating the hole. Fortunately, the radio had not been hit. We listened to the radio every afternoon before going out on patrol. We were able to pick up the Armed Forces radio station. Someone at the station had a weird sense of humor. Every afternoon they played the same song – "I Wish It Would Rain" by the Temptations. This was monsoon season. Believe me, it was raining every day.

We lived in the rain day and night. If we could find some shelter, we took it; but often we had none. We were constantly soaked. Our hands were so wrinkled from being wet that they looked like the hands of old men. We wore the same wet, dirty uniforms for weeks. It truly is amazing what a person can endure.

At times, the rain was heavy and the fog was thick. My last few days in the field hospital in Phu Bai I

The Far-Away Dream

was well enough to go out to the "outhouse" latrine. The last day when I went out the rain had stopped and the fog had lifted. There, to my surprise, not far beyond the camp was a mountain. I had not seen that mountain before because it had been hidden by the rain and the fog.

On another occasion, my squad had gone out on a patrol and had set up a small defensive perimeter for the night. Each team had one man stand watch at a time. During my watch I heard movement out in front of me; but I couldn't see anything due to the rain and fog. Then I heard voices. At the time I was the grenadier. Instead of a rifle I had a M-79 grenade launcher and a 45 pistol. I had not fired my pistol and I wasn't 100% confident that it would fire. I felt the enemy may have been too close for the rounds from the grenade launcher to explode in time. I thought of getting an M-16 rifle from either the man on my right or the one on my left; but both were asleep and had tight grips on their weapons. I fired the grenade launcher. Everyone in our position awoke and began firing in all directions. The next morning, we found some tracks in the sand where someone had been dragged away and not more than 15 feet in front of our position we found some sort of explosive and some matches. We figured someone had tried to light the explosive to toss at us and were unable to get it lit. For once we were very thankful for the rain and the extremely wet conditions.

Houston vs. UCLA

I have some very good memories as well as some horrible memories of my time in Vietnam. The Temptations were one of my favorite Motown groups, so I actually enjoyed listening to "I Wish It Would Rain" every day. I was also able to hear the first meeting that year between the UCLA and the University of Houston basketball teams played at the Astrodome. I had always been a fan of John Wooden and the UCLA Bruins as well as Red Auerbach and the Boston Celtics – of course these were the perennial champs, throughout the 50s and 60s, of college and professional basketball, respectively. Houston, led by Elvin Hayes, won that first meeting 71-69; but the Bruins, led by Lew Alcindor (better known as Kareem Abdul Jabbar) destroyed them in the rematch during the NCAA tournament: 101-69. So, it turned out well in the end.

Soda, Beer, Drugs and Sex

I liked having soda and beer delivered to us in the field. It would be brought in trailers that had started the journey with ice covering the beverage cans. But by the time it reached us it would just be wet, warm cans of beer and soda. I like beer; but I don't like it warm. However, I quickly discovered that I could trade one can of beer for two cans of soda. We were given two cans of each. I would end up with six cans of soda. I could handle that – even though the soda was warm. It reminded me of when my brother Bill and I were young and we would go to a wedding reception. We were permitted to have all the soda we could drink; and so, we would have contests to see who could drink the most. There was no doubt that I could handle six cans, and I was more than happy to do it.

Much has been written about drug use in Vietnam. This is an area in which I must confess complete ignorance. I didn't smoke cigarettes, so why would I smoke marijuana? If the other men were smoking it, I was totally unaware. Likewise, I know there were prostitutes available, even in the field; but I had no interest in them. They were often brought to our locations on the backs of motorcycles. As a matter of fact, I was glad that I had never had a serious relationship with any girl and I had no girlfriend back home. The married men and those who had steady girls were often thinking about them. I can honestly say I had few, if any, such distractions. My mind was on the task at hand.

Praying without ceasing

At the same time, my mind was a little divided. Within a few years following my time in Vietnam I saw the movie "Fiddler on the Roof." The main character, Tevye, was a very religious man who often talked to

God as he went about his routine of delivering milk and cheese. This reminded me of my own behavior in Vietnam. Whether I was on patrol, in an ambush site, or carrying out any number of other tasks, I was always talking to God – not out loud, like Tevye, but in my head, in my thoughts. I was always totally aware of what was going on around me, while also constantly talking to God. Years later when I began to learn and understand more of what is taught in the Bible, I came to discover that what I was doing is what the apostle Paul refers to as "praying without ceasing."

I had grown up attending Sunday school, worship, and, in my teens, Baptist Youth Fellowship. I was taken to church from the time I was an infant. For some reason my parents stopped attending church regularly when I was in high school. Since my church was in Rochester, Pennsylvania, and we lived on the far side of neighboring New Brighton, we were something like five or six miles away. I didn't have a driver's license until after I had graduated from high school, so every Sunday I hitchhiked to church in the morning, then back home; and again in the evening, and back home. We didn't read the Bible in my home. But I began reading the Bible in my bedroom soon after I was given my first Bible by my fourth grade Sunday school teacher, Mrs. Ellis. In our home, we only prayed on Sundays before eating dinner. I learned how to pray regularly in Marine Corps boot camp. (I would say that I got through boot camp on my knees.) This was perhaps the most valuable preparation I received for my time in Vietnam. Too bad all Marines. soldiers, sailors and airmen don't receive this training.

Leading worship

I was by no means a Bible scholar; but my parents had given me a Bible with a zippered cover to take with me to Vietnam. I had this with me always.

I only remember seeing our chaplain two or three times. On Sunday mornings, I began to invite the other men in my squad to join me for a time of worship. We would read Scripture, talk about it some, pray for each other and our families, and sing. Since we either came from different church backgrounds or, in the case of some men, no church background at all, we did not know the same hymns. But we wanted to include singing in our time of worship. So, we sang what we all knew – early Beatles songs, like "She Loves You" and "I Want to Hold Your Hand." No doubt our singing kept the enemy away. It probably drove them away. But I believe our worship truly pleased and honored the Lord. It certainly was a blessing and an encouragement to us.

The Enemy within

We still went on patrols. One day the entire platoon was on patrol. That evening we set up a large perimeter. There was a well-worn path that ran through the middle of the perimeter. My team was set up right next to where the path entered one side of the perimeter.

Just a few days before going on this patrol, our squad leader had suggested (?) that all the members of the squad should get their hair cut. He wanted us all to have our hair short – like less than ½ inch long. He was thinking this would make it easier for us to receive medical attention in the event of a head wound. All the men complied, except one. This man was relatively new to the platoon. He was not yet one of us. To prove this, he had fallen asleep on watch a few times. The squad leader was already angry at this man and agitated with me, his team leader, for his sleeping on watch. The squad leader told me to convince the man to have his hair cut. I tried. The man told me he did not want to get his hair cut so short in case he would have to go home for some emergency. He just did not want to go home practically bald.

When we were in this perimeter, as was usual, one man in each team stood watch at a time. The new man who would not get his haircut and who had fallen asleep on watch several times, was next to me and he was on watch. I must not have been sleeping very soundly (how could I, knowing this man's record?). I heard some men speaking Vietnamese inside the perimeter. They must have walked right past this man. He probably had dozed off. Then I heard him speak to them. He told them to be quiet. (He must have thought they were ARVNs – soldiers of the Army of the Republic of Vietnam, our allies. We sometimes fought with them. But there were none with us. I knew this. I guess he didn't or he was just disoriented.) As soon as he spoke to them, they opened fire and killed him. They were inside our perimeter. It was dangerous for us to fire toward them, since we could easily hit our own men on the other side of the perimeter. My squad leader and others engaged them in hand to hand combat, capturing two of them. It became clear that they had walked right through our perimeter on the path and, without realizing we were there, had stopped to rest. Their cargo was stacked near where they were found. They must have been carrying supplies from a nearby village out to their comrades.

The Museum of the Marine Corps: "Comrades"

Speaking of "comrades." Soon after the Museum of the Marine Corps was opened in Quantico, Virginia, my wife, younger children and I drove down from our home outside of Baltimore to go through the museum. I moved slower than my family and at one point my wife sent one of our sons to tell me that they had come across a picture of me. The son took me to the site, then left me to catch up with his mother and the rest of the family. I stood there looking at my photo. It was in the section devoted to the Battle of Hue. It was in front of an Ontos. It was the picture of me being treated by a corpsman when I had received shrapnel from a rocket in the Battle of Hue. I desperately wanted to show someone that picture. There was one man standing behind me. I began to talk to him. It was clear that English was not his native language. He had a very peculiar accent. I showed him the picture and told him it was me. He said, "So you were in the Battle of Hue." Then he told me, "I had many comrades in the Battle of Hue." He had been a Russian advisor for the North Vietnamese Army. I couldn't believe it. I was in the Museum of the Marine Corps. I was standing in front of a picture of me. And the only person in sight had been an advisor to the enemy. His "comrades" had killed many Marines, including members of my platoon, squad and team; and had wounded many more, including me, twice. I couldn't have been more surprised and shocked. Comrades indeed!

The Snake by Daniel Crum

Other dangers

One night my squad was on a patrol walking on a dike through a rice paddy. It was quite dark, since there was considerable cloud cover. I don't know if there was any light from the moon. Visibility was limited. We kept good spacing between us – a few yards at least. At one point I saw a snake come onto the dike in front of me. I stopped. I was carrying an M-16 rifle; but I did not want to shoot the snake and give away our position. [In guerrilla warfare training we had been instructed that there were so many species of poisonous snakes in Vietnam that the corpsmen would not be equipped to treat us if we were bitten by one. Our instructor had told us, "If you are bitten by a snake and your corpsman offers you a strong drink (you know, like whiskey), take it. This will be his way of saying there is nothing he can do for you.] This bit of instruction quickly ran through my mind. I prayed. I think the snake looked at me, shook its head from side to side, then slithered down over the far side of the dike from which it had come. I immediately moved on. This all happened in less than a minute; but time seemed to stand still until the snake was gone.

Another day we were walking on a dike through a rice paddy with a road about 50 or so yards on our left flank. Suddenly we were fired on from the right flank. Just as this happened we saw an Army convoy approaching on the road. We ran across the paddy – I think there were perpendicular dikes – and boarded the various Army vehicles. Trucks were hauling trailers with construction equipment. We boarded trailers with bulldozers and other heavy equipment. We were glad for the cover and the ride. No one had been hit.

Mrs. Stafford and Easter Sunday

I continued leading my squad – and others from the platoon who joined us – in worship each Sunday. I had not been appointed an official lay leader. I just did this on my own.

This might be a good place to mention Mrs. Stafford again. The pastor of my church in Rochester, Pennsylvania, was Pastor Jack Stafford. His son Roger was one of my best friends and I had a crush on the pastor's daughter Lois. But the most important member of the family in my life was Pastor Stafford's wife. I think her name was Eunice; but I'm not sure. I knew her as Mrs. Stafford. The day before I left for recruit training I went to visit the Staffords. Mrs. Stafford, who was truly my spiritual mother, asked me to go outside with her. There she surprised me by asking me if I had ever thought about being a minister. No one, not even her, had ever asked me that question before. At the time, I thought it was a ridiculous question. I was leaving the next day for the Marine Corps. But, then, throughout my time in boot camp, the question kept coming back to my mind. At the same time, I began to rely on the Lord like I never had before. By the fifth or sixth week of boot camp I became convinced that the Lord was calling me to the pastoral ministry. I wanted to tell someone. I asked if I could speak to the chaplain. I told the chaplain I thought I had received a call to the ministry. The chaplain thought I was seeking a way out of the Marine Corps. I assured him I was not. I told him plainly that I had pledged four years of my life to my country; but that I was giving the remainder of my life, including these four years, to serve my Lord.

The Marine Corps had not commissioned me as a lay leader in my platoon; but I believe the Lord had, though I did not think about it in that way at the time. It was now April; and Easter was approaching. I was asked if I would lead worship for the entire platoon on Easter. (It may even have been for the entire company.) I was nervous about this; but I was willing to do it. However, to my surprise and delight, the chaplain showed up on Easter Sunday. He invited me to participate, but, of course he led the worship. This was one of only a few times I remember seeing him. But I was extremely glad he had come.

Before I move on, I should also note that I visited the Stafford home again near the end of my time at home before going to California for Guerilla Warfare Training, then on to Vietnam. Mrs. Stafford had grown up in a missionary family. Her family had served somewhere in Asia and she had received from her mother the practice of placing Bible verses in fortune cookies and giving these to guests. When her husband had come to propose to her, his fortune cookie had read, "For He will deliver you from the snare of the fowler." – Psalm 91:3. Mrs. Stafford's maiden name was Fowler. The cookie Mrs. Stafford gave to me yielded a verse that read, "A thousand may fall at your side, ten thousand at your right hand; but it will not come near you." – Psalm 91:7. How I thank the Lord for Mrs. Stafford's love as well as for the Lord's preservation of my life.

Booby Traps & Grenades; Wounded for the Third Time

Shortly after Easter we were sent to an area that was like a desert – it was mostly sand with very few trees, though there were occasional clumps of trees, like an oasis. We had very few encounters with the enemy during this time, but we did come across several booby-trapped mines. They were scattered throughout the area. They were practically undetectable. We had to move very cautiously.

One night we had bivouacked (camped, for you civilians) in one of those clumps of trees. This one was rather large. I was watching one Marine as he walked off alone. I saw him get behind a tree, take out a grenade, stick out his leg, then toss the grenade to the side of the tree where only his leg was exposed. He told the corpsman that he had tripped a mine. I saw this Marine a week or so later at a hospital on Guam. His injury was worse than he had planned. He had ruptured his spleen. I had thought of reporting what I had seen, but now decided this was punishment enough. I kept what I knew to myself. No doubt it was clear even to the corpsman that the injury was not caused by a mine but that it was self-inflicted. I discovered in the Guam hospital that this was not uncommon.

Sometime in the next few days we were on a patrol through this "desert" when we were fired upon from our right flank. We began to run for cover. My best friend at the time was right in front of me. I saw him trip and I immediately knew what that meant. He had tripped a mine. There would be a brief delay and the mine would explode. There was nothing I could do. The mine exploded right underneath me. It lifted me into the air. Inexplicably, I landed on my feet. I was standing there for a while – once again time stood still. I was holding my rifle. A pack was on my back. I was weighed down with ammunition, canteens, hand grenades, you name it … And I stood there. Then I told myself to just lie down. I fell backwards on my pack.

The Far-Away Dream

A piece of shrapnel had entered my neck and was pressing against my windpipe. (God had stopped it from penetrating my windpipe.) I was having a hard time breathing and tried to yank the piece out. Another friend did yank it out. At last I could breathe. Now I noticed my more serious wounds. I started screaming, "My balls, my balls are gone!" The same friend who had removed the shrapnel from my neck pulled on the belt of my trousers and reported, "Crum, you're okay!" I shouted, "You liar. There's so much blood, there is no way you can tell!" And I continued screaming.

A helicopter soon arrived. I was placed on a stretcher and was being carried to the helicopter. Those carrying me must have been sinking and slipping in the sand. I was being bounced around on the stretcher. I was yelling at them. All at once I thought, "They're doing the best they can. Why don't you just pass out?" The next thing I remember is waking up in a hospital bed.

When I woke up in that hospital bed there seemed to be tubes coming out from every part of me. Suddenly, I remembered, "My balls?" I was covered by a sheet. At once I summoned all the strength I could muster and I lifted that sheet and raised my head, examining my mid-section. I sighed a huge sigh of relief. My friend had told the truth. Everything was there. I fell back into a very restful sleep.

"That Purple Heart I was hoping for"

I had two visitors while I was lying in that bed. One was my friend who had tripped the mine. He had come to cheer me up. "Hey Crum," he said with a large grin on his face, "you know that mine that blew you to bits? Well, I got a piece in the back of my head and now I have that Purple Heart I was hoping for." I don't often think in thoughts that contain profanity – as you can probably tell from this memoir – but this was one time that was an exception to that rule. I thought, "You dumb shit! You trip a mine that practically kills me and you come celebrating the fact that you finally have a Purple Heart because of some scratch on the back of your head?" He was laughing. I was too weak to even express myself. Although the more I thought about it after he left, I was glad he had gotten his much-desired Purple Heart without sustaining a more serious wound or death.

Now why would someone want a Purple Heart so badly?

One day in the field, following the Battle of Hue, we had a company formation in which an officer gave out medals to some who had fought in the battle. This friend of mine had not been with us in Hue. I was one of the men being given a medal. Mine was the Purple Heart. [If you have never seen the Purple Heart medal, it is purple with a gold silhouette of

The Far-Away Dream

George Washington in the middle; and the purple area is bordered by a gold heart. It really is a very impressive medal.] I had been wounded twice in Hue, but you are only supposed to be awarded one Purple Heart medal (this may be true for all medals, I don't know). Additional "awards" of the medal are indicated by stars placed on the medal. (More about this later.) Although this friend had not been in the Battle of Hue, he was in the field with us when we received our medals. He told me that day that this was the one medal he wanted and he told me why.

His father had been a career Navy officer and, I believe, he still was in the Navy while we were serving in Vietnam. My friend thought the one thing that would impress his dad was his being wounded in combat. Receiving the Purple Heart, without dying, would be the proof that he had suffered a combat wound. It would be his "red badge of courage," even if it was purple and gold. I was lying in a hospital bed with serious wounds in my right arm, my right shoulder, and my stomach, and a minor wound in my neck. I could hardly move and could barely talk. But he had his Purple Heart. And, as it turned out, I had my ticket out of Vietnam. It could have been worse.

Double Prizes by Zion Crum

The Far-Away Dream

A second Purple Heart medal

This brings me to my second visitor in that hospital bed.

An officer came around pinning Purple Hearts on all the patients. In the first place, I did not know that once you had been given one, you were not supposed to be given another one. In the second place, I really did not know what was going on – thanks, I'm sure, to that wonderful pain-numbing and mind-altering drug, morphine. And thirdly, I could barely talk. The officer spoke to me. I am not sure I said anything to him, let alone, "No thanks, sir, I already have one of those." So, as it turned out, I ended up with two Purple Heart medals.

After a few days in that hospital – I think it may have been the field hospital in Phu Bai – I was transferred to a hospital in Danang. This was an Air Force hospital. I imagine it was the regular last stop before the seriously wounded were flown out of country. An Air Force medic – for some reason the Army and Air Force have medics and the Navy and Marine Corps have corpsmen – at any rate, an Air Force medic asked me if I had received my scheduled shot of morphine. (I imagine the Air Force medical field uses charts for their patients. But what do I know? He asked me if I had received my shot. He did not consult any chart.) I told him I had not. For whatever reason – maybe I already loved the high I got from morphine – I lied. I had been given a shot just a few minutes earlier.

He left and returned with my injection. He asked me where I wanted it. I pointed to one of my arms. Surprised he pointed out what a long needle he was holding. I said something about being a Marine and I wouldn't feel it. (Not to mention the fact that I had just had a shot and I wasn't feeling anything.) He got into some karate-like position and prepared to administer the shot. I asked what in the world he was doing. He said that he had had Marines react before by attacking him. I was practically immobile and was still filled with tubes. How could I possibly attack him? But then again, I was a Marine. You never can tell. He gave me the shot. I guess it could have killed me. But I sure did feel good!

Good-Bye Vietnam!

While I was still experiencing the high from the additional morphine I was transferred to an airplane for my flight out of Vietnam. What a way to fly! We were stacked on this Medivac plane like cargo, with stretchers 3 or 4 or more high. Somewhere on the flight the morphine wore off. The plane may have been flying, but I was at an all-time low. The pain was severe. We landed. I think we had flown to the Philippines. Some of the wounded were taken off the plane, others were put in their places. Each of us had some sort of tag. I noticed someone doing something with my tag. I could reach around my head and grab it. It had read CONUS. But there was now a line through that word with the word GUAM written beside it. Originally, I had been scheduled to fly to the Continental United States – home; but now I was being sent to the island of Guam. I figured that out later, but for the time being, this was one more thing I did not know and did not understand.

Guam: Quiet and Safe

There was a major Naval Hospital on Guam; but there was also a small hospital annex, located on a beach. I was taken to the annex. I don't remember the trip there; but I do remember waking up there. Something seemed strange. Before long I realized what it was. For the first time in months I could not hear the sounds of war. I was truly out of Vietnam. I was seriously wounded; but I was alive. To this day Guam is one of my favorite places on earth.

The hospital annex, it turned out, was something like a nudist camp. But, instead of walking around naked, we walked, were wheeled, or limped around in pajamas. The annex was on the beach. It included several hospital wards, a mess hall (or dining room), a club (bar), a few other buildings, a basketball court and an outdoor theater with bench seating, as well as spots for wheel chairs. We would sit watching a movie, those well enough to be permitted entrance to the club would sneak six-packs of beer to the rest of us (for some reason I don't think this was monitored very closely), and we enjoyed Clint Eastwood in "The Good, the Bad and the Ugly," or Omar Sharif and Julie Christie in "Dr. Zhivago." I remember while we were watching "Dr. Zhivago" someone called out that a storm was approaching across the ocean. (On Guam, you could see a storm approaching ten or fifteen minutes before it would arrive.) No one moved. The storm came, we got soaked, the storm passed on, we watched the end of the movie, and when we returned to our wards the corpsmen were waiting for us, handing out clean, dry pajamas.

Another wonderful feature about being a patient at the annex was that every other week a bus would load up with men to be taken to a nearby restaurant. The owner of the restaurant was himself a veteran who treated as many as could fit on his bus to a free dinner. The dinner included salad, pizza, spaghetti, soft drinks, and girls from the college of Guam to keep us company. Now who could ever forget that?

What I found sad about my stay in the hospital was that many of the men would be sent back to Vietnam once their wounds were healed. I would not be sent back

The Far-Away Dream

since I had been wounded three times. Two men, who would be sent back, became good friends of mine while we were in the hospital. Both were fellow Marines. One was from Detroit and the other was from Flint, Michigan. One of them was in the hospital as the result of a self-inflicted wound. I still have a letter I received from him. It was written at a time when he should have been home, but he was still in Vietnam because he was serving extra time as payment for the time he had spent in the hospital. This was part of his punishment for the self-inflicted wound.

I could have signed a waiver and then I would have been sent back. I did give this some thought, since my fellow Marines were still there. But then I decided this would not be fair to my mother (three notices that her son had been injured were certainly as much as she should have had to endure). I would not go back. Instead I was sent to Okinawa to complete the remainder of my 13 months tour of duty overseas. And so, the Vietnam chapter of my life, a short but eventful chapter, ended. Although I can still remember vividly some of the details, it often does not seem to me that it really happened. It seems more like something I saw in a movie or in a far-away dream.

Chapter Four

Life after Vietnam

An excellent wife, who can find? For her worth is far above jewels.

— Proverbs 31:10

Behold, children are a gift of the Lord, the fruit of the womb is a reward.

— Psalm 127:3

Some wonderful Post Vietnam assignments

Post-Vietnam has now grown to nearly fifty years. Much has happened in that time. As far as my Marine Corps experience is concerned, I could not have asked for a better or more satisfying time. On Okinawa, I became a military policeman (MP) at Camp Hansen, a small Marine Corps base. Then I was transferred to the Armed Forces Police, in which Marines served with soldiers, sailors and airman (Army, Navy and Air

Force) patrolling the towns where servicemen went on liberty (their free time off base). We did our best to keep these men (and a small number of servicewomen) out of trouble. I used to laugh thinking my mother was relieved that I was now out of harm's way, since I was no longer in Vietnam. She would have been shocked to know how often I was engaged in another sort of warfare waged in the bars and on the streets between Army Green Beret and Marines, drunken sailors and drunken airmen. I loved it. I especially valued the opportunity to deliver intoxicated and very vulnerable Marines back to their barracks. I had learned how to wake up those who had passed out when their buddies could not. But once I woke them, I refused to leave them in the bars; I took them back to their barracks, where they could then sleep in the comfort and safety of their bunks.

When my overseas tour ended, I was assigned to the Marine Corps Base at Quantico, Virginia. At that time, to my knowledge, there was no Military Police MOS (military occupational specialty) in the Marine Corps. Men from other specialties would simply be selected to serve as MPs. My MOS was infantry rifleman. When I arrived at Quantico I had no specific orders as to what I would be doing there. The woman checking me in reviewed my records and saw that I had served as an MP and in the Armed Forces Police on Okinawa; so, she asked if I wanted to be assigned to the Military Police

The Far-Away Dream

at Quantico. I thought about it briefly, then said no. She turned her head and looked out the window and asked, "How do you like humping hills?" (Quantico is where the Marine Corps has its Office Training School (OCS). OCS is even more physically demanding than the basic training enlisted men like myself undergo. And guess who takes these officer candidates through their field training in the hills of Quantico: infantry riflemen like me.) I promptly declared, "I'll be an MP!" She made some notations on my orders, gave me some directions, and sent me off to the Military Police station.

I served as an MP at Quantico for six or seven months, then I was moved into the Investigation branch. I was made an Accident Investigator. You may remember my noting earlier that I "may hold the record for holding the rank of E-1/Private the longest." The flip side of this is that it is hard to imagine anyone moving from Lance Corporal to Sergeant quicker than I did. I was promoted from Lance Corporal to Corporal in the Spring or Summer of 1969. I was a Corporal when I began to work as an investigator. The Provost Marshall (military for Chief of Police) did not think it was appropriate for corporals to be investigators; thus, I was promoted to Sergeant sometime in the Fall or early Winter of 69. I was a Corporal, I believe, for less time than I had been a Private.

The Provost Marshall wanted me to become a Criminal Investigator. I was assigned OJT (on the job training) with a criminal investigator; but to become one myself I needed to be sent to the Army criminal investigation school; and for this to happen, I would have had to reenlist for another three or four years. I had not lost sight of what I believed to be a call to the ministry. (You may recall that I had told the chaplain in boot camp that I had pledged four years of my life to my country; but that I was giving the remainder of my life, including these four years, to serve my Lord.) I was determined to complete my present enlistment then pursue that calling. And so instead of reenlisting I was granted an early out (as were many others who had already served tours in Vietnam). I had enlisted for four years. I was released from active duty at the end of May in 1970. I had served two years and 10 months. My time in the Marine Corps came to an abrupt ending.

Post USMC: The Early Years

It was early June 1970 when I was a civilian once again. I needed a place to live. I returned home. Soon I discovered that my dad considered going to college a waste of time, regardless of any sense of calling I claimed to have to the ministry. Before long I returned to the apprentice job at St. Joe Lead. However, I stayed there for less than a month. I quit and began looking for a college to attend in the Fall. Demonstrating how little I knew about colleges, I settled on a state college in the panhandle of West Virginia. I chose it because it was not more than a two-hour drive away. I had no idea that I could have gone to a state college in Pennsylvania and be charged in-state fees. In West Virginia I had to pay out-of-state fees. On the other hand, I was accepted immediately and could begin without delay. In late August, I entered West Liberty State College, outside of Wheeling, West Virginia.

After a one-week struggle to convince myself I belonged in college, I settled in and once again was a good student. I did so well my first semester that I was awarded an educational program by the Veterans' Administration called Vocational Rehabilitation. I qualified for this program because I had been given a rating of 50% disability, due to the injuries suffered in Vietnam. This meant I could afford to go to the college of my choice. I chose to go to a small Christian college north of Boston near the Massachusetts coast. Gordon College is the college Pastor Stafford had attended and both his son and his daughter were there at the time. I left West Liberty and headed to New England and the beautiful campus of Gordon College. This was the first in what became a long list of benefits I would receive for having been injured in Vietnam.

David & Jill

Marriage and Family

Speaking of benefits, in addition to a wonderful, practically all-expenses-paid education I received at Gordon, it was there that I also met my wife. To be specific we encountered one another on one of the first days of our time at Gordon, although we did not realize it until about a year later. My time at Gordon did nothing but confirm my sense of call to the ministry. I spent a summer in short-term missions in northwestern Canada, I served as president of the Campus Mission Project (CMP), and I grew in my faith and in my commitment to the Lord Jesus Christ.

Much of my spiritual growth during college sprang from my relationship to a certain Jill Moir. While I had grown up attending Sunday school and worship at my church in Rochester, Pennsylvania, and while I certainly had faith in Jesus Christ as a Marine, I was still quite lacking in Biblical knowledge and I was woefully ignorant of Biblical theology. Jill had been raised attending a small church in Basking Ridge, New Jersey, a stone's throw from her home in Bernardsville, where her pastor, Dale Crouthamel, fresh out of seminary, taught the adult Sunday school class what he had recently learned himself. Because the church was so small, as a teen, Jill attended the adult class. She received, in my estimation, a seminary education in Biblical theology while she was in high school. And she was more than happy to share her knowledge with me. (At first it felt like she was force-feeding me; but in time, I came to appreciate what I was receiving.)

Jill Moir and I married exactly one week after graduating with our Bachelor degrees. During our pre-marriage counseling with Pastor Wendall Rockey, the pastor of the church we attended while at Gordon, we came to the subject of "family planning." Jill and I told Pastor Rockey we wanted to discuss this and pray about it ourselves before hearing what he had to say. We read some books and we perused the Bible on the subject. We both were deeply impressed with how the Bible refers to children as "a gift from the Lord" and how it speaks of a man being blessed "whose quiver is full of them" and the wife being "like a fruitful vine" – Psalms 127 and 128. We couldn't think of anything else described in the Bible as a blessing that people would say, "I only want so much of it." We decided we would gladly receive as many "blessings" as the Lord would decide to give us. We would leave the "family planning" to God. Pastor Rockey deferred to our decision. Little did we know that the Lord would bless us with eleven children; and with each new child the Lord blessed us with increased faith in His sovereignty and goodness.

Jill and I graduated from Gordon on May 24, 1975, and we were joined in matrimony on May 31st. (Jill did not want to be a June bride. Good thing May 31st was a Saturday, or we may have had to wait until July to be married.) Instead of heading straight to seminary to prepare for the ministry, we headed south to Florida and teaching positions at a private Christian school. I thought that one of the most important roles of a pastor was that of teacher and that a couple years of teaching was the best way to prepare for pastoral ministry.

I should mention, however, that we did not go directly to Florida from college. First, we had a summer job at a yacht club on Cape Cod. Now that was one tremendous way to begin our married life: summer on Cape Cod, then off to the Sunshine State for the remainder of our first year together. We taught at Lakeland Christian School in Lakeland, Florida, for two wonderful years, then we were off to Philadelphia where I entered Westminster Theological Seminary and where God began to bless us with children.

A Navy Chaplain

When Peter David arrived in October 1977 we had no idea that he would be followed by nine more sons and one daughter. But that is what happened. While still in seminary, but now at Reformed Episcopal Seminary in west Philadelphia, Matthew (1979) and Benjamin (1981) joined Peter. I received an appointment as a chaplain in the Navy in 1982 with an initial assignment to Camp Pendleton Marine Corps Base on the California coast, north of San Diego and south of Los Angeles. Jonathan

(1983) and Nathaniel (1985) were born while we were at Camp Pendleton; Jon while I served at the Infantry Training School, Nate while I was chaplain of the 2nd Battalion, 7th Marines (7th Marine Regiment).

From Camp Pendleton, we headed north to Mare Island, California, just north of San Francisco. While on Mare Island I served at the chapel at Hamilton Air Base, not far from the Golden Gate Bridge, and at St. Peter's Chapel on Mare Island. Thomas (1987) was born during this time at nearby Travis Air Force Base. My next and last assignment was on a nuclear aircraft carrier, the USS Carl Vinson. Since it was homeported in Alameda, across the bay from San Francisco, we could keep our house on Mare Island. This allowed Jill and the children to remain in a familiar place surrounded by friends we had made, while I went to sea. It also meant Jill and the children were there, and I was at sea, when the deadly earthquake struck the Bay area at the start of the World Series between the Oakland Athletics and the San Francisco Giants in 1989.

A Pastor at Last

At the very end of 1989 we left California and headed, with baby in womb, for St. Louis. I had decided it would be best to prepare further for pastoral ministry (sensing it was much different from military chaplaincy) and so I had begun studies in the Doctor of Ministry program of

Covenant Theological Seminary. Although participation in the Doctor of Ministry courses did not require residency at or near the seminary, we had no place else to go, so we went to St. Louis. It was there that David (1990) was born. In 1991, I received a call to serve as pastor of Covenant Presbyterian Church in Landisville, Pennsylvania (just outside of Lancaster). Off we went to Lancaster County. Stephen (1993) arrived while we lived in Landisville. He was delivered by a mid-wife. Most of the mid-wife's clients were Amish. Nevertheless, Stephen prefers hot cars to horse and buggies.

Our first daughter, and the only one born to us, was our first Hoosier. Jill Elisabeth (1994) made her appearance soon after we arrived in Bloomington, Indiana. We had come to Bloomington so that I could serve as an associate pastor at Evangelical Community Church (ECC). It was exciting to be in a college town (Bloomington is the home of Indiana University) and to be part of a rather large church with a substantial student presence. (When Jill was born, to avoid having people ask us if we were now finished having children – you know, we now had our girl – I announced to the congregation the birth of our "first" daughter. Little did I know she would be our only daughter, except for all those who would marry our sons.)

I left ECC in 1996 and, at the encouragement of Pastor Tim Bayly, began a ministry in Bloomington to help people find freedom from homosexuality through

The Crum Children

faith in and dependence upon Jesus Christ. This ministry provided the foundation for my doctoral thesis and was beautifully used of the Lord in the lives of some very dear men and women. During this time, William (1997) and Jesse (1999) were also born in Bloomington.

In 2000 I had a yearning to return to pastoral ministry. I received a call to serve as Senior Pastor of Westminster Presbyterian Church in Brandon, Florida, just to the east of Tampa. Not only were no children born while we were in Brandon (Jesse was the last of our children), we left three children behind in Bloomington and Peter had already gone to work in Colorado. Our family was shrinking. We only had six sons and one daughter with us when we moved to Florida. In 2006 we left Florida for Catonsville, Maryland – a suburb of Baltimore. By then we were down to four sons and one daughter in tow. After nine years at Bishop Cummins Reformed Episcopal Church in Catonsville, I decided it was time to retire and Jill was more than ready to live near most of our children and grandchildren.

We moved back to Bloomington, Indiana, accompanied by our last two sons, William and Jesse. Now we are just a short drive from all but one of our other children and all but three of our grandchildren. Peter and his wife, Jess, and their three children, Jude, Ashley and Aravis live in Colorado, and will soon be moving to Florida. Living here in Bloomington are Matt and Emily with their two sons, Landon and Levi; Ben

The Crum Clan

and Michal, and their sons, Daniel, Zion and Knox, and their daughter, Clementine; Jon and Tenile, and their sons, Phinehas and Abel, and their daughters, Cecilia and Flannery; Nate and Katie, and their sons, Ezra and Matthias, and their daughter, Abigail; Stephen (still single); John and Jill Elisabeth and their son, Max; and William and Jesse. Thomas and Alyssa live a little over an hour away in Indianapolis with their two sons, Titus and Theodore; and David, still single but engaged, also lives in Indianapolis. As of this writing my wife Jill and I have 19 grandchildren with two others already being formed in their mother's womb.

Postlude

The mind of man plans his way, but the Lord directs his steps.

– Proverbs 16:9

I enlisted in the Marine Corps to get away from working in a mill. That was my reason. God directed me to join the Marine Corps so that He could form me into the man He intended I would be.

I needed to be placed in a situation in which I would learn to lean upon the Lord. For me, this was, first of all, recruit training at Parris Island, South Carolina. I also needed the guidance that would lead me to lean upon Him and not to trust in my own capability. This came through Mrs. Stafford's question, "Dave, have you ever thought about being a minister?"; as well as through her modeling for me what it means to truly love the Lord and to trust in Him.

The Marine Corps did its best to prepare me for Vietnam; and I think it did an excellent job. And yet the most critical preparation came from my learning to pray about all things, all the time, regardless of where I was or what I was doing. God had called me to Himself. He had filled me with faith in Him. I knew Jesus Christ as my Lord and Savior in a very personal way. I was so immersed in the life I had in Christ that, surrounded by death, I hardly thought about it and never feared it.

On the other hand, while God has richly blessed me before, during, and after my time in the Marine Corps, I have often failed Him in many ways. It is not some sort of noteworthy humility that has me admit my failures and sins; it is reluctant honesty.

I have loved my wife, but I have often been unloving toward her: unkind and unfaithful (in my mind if not in physical adultery). I have loved our sons and daughter, but I have often been mean to them and distant (sometimes physically, such as when I was deployed as a chaplain; but other times simply not giving them the attention they needed). I have often failed my family and the people I have served as a chaplain and as a pastor by my self-centeredness and my laziness.

My sin and my failures are real; so is God's grace, love and forgiveness. I treasure passages of Scripture such as 1 John 1:8-10: *If we say we have no sin, we are deceiving ourselves and the truth is not in us. If we confess our sins, He is faithful and righteous to forgive us our sins and to cleanse us from all unrighteousness. If we say we have not sinned, we make Him a liar and His word in not in us.* Ephesians 2:1-9: *And you were dead in your trespasses and sins, in which you formerly walked ... But God, being rich in mercy ... made us alive together with Christ ... For by grace you have been saved through faith; and that not of yourselves, it is the gift of God; not as a result of works, so that no one may boast.* And Romans 8:38-39: *For I am convinced that neither death, nor life, nor angels, nor principalities, nor things present, nor things to come, nor powers, nor height, nor depth, nor any other created thing, will be able to separate us from the love of God, which is in Christ Jesus our Lord.*

This makes me think of another, much more tremendous far-away dream; and as my dream of having been in Vietnam is a memory of what really happened, this dream is also based on reality – on ultimate reality. It is the dream, the longing, the sure hope that one day I will be with the Lord; not because of anything I have done or could do, but because of what Christ has done for me, in taking upon Himself my sin and suffering the penalty for my sin by dying on the cross. As one of my favorite hymns proclaims, "My hope is built on nothing less than Jesus' blood and righteousness. I dare not trust the sweetest frame, but wholly lean on Jesus' name." And so, I will end this account of mine with one of my very favorite verses of Scripture and my prayer for you. *Now may the God of hope fill you with all joy and peace in believing, so that you will abound in hope by the power of the Holy Spirit.* (Romans 15:13)

Glossary

Enlisted Marine Corps ranking and abbreviations used in this book:

> Private (Pvt) – the lowest enlisted rank
> Private First Class (PFC) – rank above Private
> Lance Corporal (LCpl) – rank above Private First Class
> Corporal (Cpl) – rank above Lance Corporal
> Sergeant (Sgt) – rank above Corporal
> Staff Sergeant (SSgt) – rank above Sergeant
> Gunnery Sergeant (GySgt, also referred to as Gunny) – rank above Staff Sergeant
> Sergeant Major – the highest enlisted rank

Officer Marine Corps ranking and abbreviations used in this book:

> Second Lieutenant (2nd Lt.) – lowest officer rank, not including Warrant Officers
> Lieutenant Colonel (LtCol) – 4 ranks above 2nd Lt., often referred to as Colonel

Colonel (Col) – rank above Lieutenant Colonel and below General

General: in ascending order:
    Brigadier General
    Lieutenant General
    Major General
    General

Marine Corps recruit training is often referred to as Boot Camp

I became a Navy Chaplain because I wanted to serve the Marine Corps. The Marine Corps comes under the Department of the Navy and is served by Navy chaplains and Navy healthcare, which includes doctors, nurses and corpsmen.

The Marine Corps infantry structure from bottom to top is (to the best of my knowledge):

Infantryman
Fire team – 4 Infantrymen
Squad – 3 Fire teams, plus squad leader & radio man
Platoon – 3 Squads, plus Platoon commander, platoon sergeant, radio man, corpsman
Company – 3 Rifle Platoons, 1 Weapons Platoon (consisting of mortars, machine guns, etc.), Company commander, company Gunnery Sergeant, radio man & others

Battalion – 4 Rifle Companies in combat, 1 Weapons Company, 1 Headquarters & Support Company, Battalion Commander & Executive Officer, battalion Sergeant Major & others

Regiment – look it up, if you want to know

Division – look it up, if you want to know

Corps – includes all the above & others, including Commandant & Sergeant Major of the Corps